LangGraph

A Comprehensive Guide to Building Agentic and Multi-agent Applications for Advanced AI Workflows

Written by
Morgan Devline

Copyright

LangGraph: A Comprehensive Guide to Building Agentic and Multi-Agent Applications for Advanced AI Workflows
Copyright © 2024 Morgan Devline
All Rights Reserved.

No part of this book may be reproduced, distributed, or transmitted in any form or by any means, including photocopying, recording, or other electronic or mechanical methods, without the prior written permission of the publisher, except in the case of brief quotations embodied in critical reviews and certain other non-commercial uses permitted by copyright law.

Disclaimer

The information provided in this book is for educational purposes only. While every effort has been made to ensure accuracy, the author and publisher make no warranties regarding the content. Readers are advised to use their discretion and consult relevant professionals for specific advice.

The author and publisher disclaim any liability for any damage or loss incurred as a result of using the information provided in this book.

All trademarks, service marks, product names, and logos used in this book are the property of their respective owners. The use of these names does not imply any endorsement by or affiliation with the owners.

Dedication

This book is dedicated to those advancing the future of AI through collaboration and innovation

Table of content

Part I: Introduction and Foundations 8

Chapter 1: Introduction to LangGraph 9
- 1.1 What is LangGraph? 9
- 1.2 History and Evolution of LangGraph 9
- 1.3 Why LangGraph Matters for Advanced AI Workflows 10
- 1.4 Key Features of LangGraph 11
- 1.5 Overview of Agentic and Multi-agent Systems 11
- 1.6 How LangGraph Fits into the LangChain Ecosystem 12

Chapter 2: The Foundations of Agentic and Multi-agent Systems .. 16
- 2.1 Understanding Agentic Workflows 16
- 2.2 Defining Multi-agent Systems 17
- 2.3 Real-World Applications of Agentic AI 17
- 2.4 Challenges Addressed by LangGraph 20

Chapter 3: Getting Started with LangGraph 23
- 3.1 Installation and Setup 23
- 3.2 Overview of LangGraph API 24
- 3.3 Your First LangGraph Workflow 25
- 3.4 Debugging Initial Setups 27
- 3.5 Hands-on Exercises: Building Basic Graphs 28

Chapter 5: Persistence and State Management in LangGraph 32
- 5.1 Understanding State Persistence 32
- 5.2 Saving and Loading Graph States 32
- 5.3 Error Recovery and Retry Mechanisms 35
- 5.4 Long-Running Tasks and Pausing Execution 38

Chapter 6: Human-in-the-Loop Systems 41
- 6.1 Designing Workflows with Human Oversight 41
- 6.2 Interrupting Execution for Human Input 42

6.3 Real-World Applications of Human-in-the-Loop AI 44

6.4 Best Practices for Collaborative Workflows 48

Chapter 7: Cycles, Branching, and Advanced Workflow Design 50

7.1 Implementing Cyclic Graphs 50

7.2 Conditional Logic and Branching 52

7.3 Error Propagation in Complex Workflows 56

7.4 Managing Dependencies in Multi-Agent Applications 57

Chapter 8: Streaming Outputs and Real-Time Feedback 60

8.1 Token-by-Token Streaming Explained 60

8.2 Enhancing User Experience with Real-Time Feedback 62

8.3 Streaming Outputs in Multi-Agent Systems 65

Chapter 9: Integration with LangChain and External Tools 70

9.1 Using LangChain Tools within LangGraph 70

9.2 API Integrations and External Dependencies 72

9.3 Combining LangGraph with Cloud Platforms 75

Chapter 10: Optimization and Performance Tuning 79

10.1 Scaling LangGraph Workflows 79

10.2 Performance Benchmarks for Large Graphs 81

10.3 Caching Mechanisms and Intelligent Resource Usage 83

10.4 Optimizing Task Queues for Parallel Execution 85

Chapter 11: Debugging and Error Handling in LangGraph 88

11.1 Common Errors and How to Fix Them 88

11.2 Visual Debugging Tools for Graphs 91

11.3 Logging and Monitoring Graph Execution 93

11.4 Best Practices for Robust Workflow Design 95

Chapter 12: DevOps and Deployment with LangGraph 97

12.1 CI/CD Pipelines for LangGraph Applications 97

12.2 Containerization with Docker and Kubernetes 100

12.3 Monitoring and Observability Tools 103

12.4 Automated Testing and Rollback Strategies 104

Chapter 13: Building Conversational Agents with LangGraph 107

13.1 Overview of Multi-Agent Conversational Workflows 107

13.2 Handling Dialog States and Persistence 108

13.3 Error Recovery in Conversational Systems 110

Chapter 14: Task Automation with LangGraph 117

14.1 Automating Complex Workflows 117

14.2 Examples: Enterprise Task Automation Scenarios 119

14.3 Managing Dependencies and Scheduling 121

Chapter 15: Custom LLM-Powered Applications 125

15.1 Building LLM-Based Recommendation Systems 125

15.2 Personalizing User Interactions with LangGraph 128

15.3 Real-Time Data Processing and Decision Making 132

Chapter 16: Case Studies: LangGraph in Action 135

16.1 Enterprise Workflow Optimization 135

16.2 Enhancing Customer Support with Multi-Agent Systems . 138

16.3 Multi-Step Task Automation in Healthcare 142

Chapter 17: Best Practices for Designing LangGraph Workflows .. 147

17.1 Modular Design for Reusability 147

17.2 Avoiding Common Pitfalls in Workflow Design 149

17.3 Security and Compliance in LangGraph Applications 151

Chapter 18: Scaling and Deployment Strategies 155

18.1 Deploying LangGraph Applications in Production 155

18.2 Horizontal Scaling for High-Volume Workflows 158

18.3 Monitoring and Iterating on Deployed Graphs 162

Chapter 19: The Future of LangGraph and Multi-Agent Systems . 165

19.1 Emerging Trends in Workflow Automation 165

19.2 How LangGraph is Shaping Agentic AI 168

19.3 Predictions for AI-Driven Workflow Systems 171

Appendix A: LangGraph API Reference 174
   20.1 Detailed API Documentation 174
   20.2 Key Classes and Methods Explained 174
Appendix B: Glossary of Terms 182
   21.1 Definitions of Core Concepts 182
   21.2 Terminology Related to LangChain and Multi-agent AI 183
Appendix C: Troubleshooting Guide 189
   22.1 Common Issues and Resolutions 189
   22.2 FAQs for LangGraph Users 193
Appendix D: Online Resources and Community Support 196
   23.1 Links to Tutorials and Code Repositories 196
   23.2 Community Forums and Discussion Groups 198
   23.3 Staying Updated on LangGraph Developments 199

Chapter 1: Introduction to LangGraph

1.1 What is LangGraph?

LangGraph is a powerful open-source framework designed to build stateful, multi-agent workflows powered by Large Language Models (LLMs). At its core, LangGraph allows developers to organize tasks into interconnected nodes and edges, creating structured workflows that are efficient, maintainable, and scalable. It stands out by enabling:

- **Agentic Systems**: LangGraph supports workflows where agents (autonomous AI units) perform complex tasks collaboratively.

- **Persistence**: Workflows can save and reload their state, enabling advanced features like error recovery and task resumption.

- **Cyclic and Branching Logic**: Unlike traditional Directed Acyclic Graphs (DAGs), LangGraph supports loops and branches, making workflows more dynamic.

Key Benefits:

- Simplifies the creation of workflows that require multiple agents.

- Enhances efficiency by supporting advanced graph structures and state management.

- Integrates seamlessly with LangChain, enabling extended functionality with LLM tools.

1.2 History and Evolution of LangGraph

LangGraph was created by LangChain Inc. as an evolution of workflow management tools to address the limitations of static systems like Directed Acyclic Graphs (DAGs). Traditional DAGs

excel in fixed workflows but struggle with dynamic requirements like retries, human interaction, and loops.
LangGraph was developed to fill this gap by:

- Enabling **state persistence** for long-running and resumable workflows.

- Supporting **cyclic graphs** for iterative processes.

- Providing out-of-the-box **human-in-the-loop** integration for workflows requiring human intervention.

With its release, LangGraph quickly gained traction among developers building complex AI-powered systems, from customer support chatbots to enterprise automation tools.

1.3 Why LangGraph Matters for Advanced AI Workflows

AI workflows often involve multiple steps that require coordination, persistence, and adaptability. For example:

1. An AI assistant retrieving data from APIs.

2. Processing data with multiple agents.

3. Logging results and restarting on failure.

LangGraph simplifies these scenarios by offering:

- **Stateful Execution**: Workflows can remember their progress and resume from the last checkpoint.

- **Error Handling**: Automatic retries and manual intervention make workflows robust.

- **Dynamic Graphs**: Incorporate real-time decision-making, branching, and loops.

Real-world impact:

- Reduces development time for multi-agent systems.

- Provides a flexible framework for designing complex workflows.

1.4 Key Features of LangGraph

1. **Nodes and Edges**: The building blocks of workflows. Each node represents a task, and edges define the flow between tasks.

2. **State Persistence**: Save and load workflow states to allow error recovery and process resumption.

3. **Cyclic Workflows**: Implement loops for iterative tasks like model retraining or feedback refinement.

4. **Human-in-the-Loop Systems**: Pause execution for manual approval or input.

5. **Streaming Outputs**: Support for real-time feedback, such as token-by-token generation.

6. **Integration with LangChain**: Access LangChain's tools and features to enhance your workflows.

1.5 Overview of Agentic and Multi-agent Systems

Agentic and multi-agent systems are AI frameworks where multiple autonomous agents collaborate to perform tasks.

- **Agentic Systems**:
  Individual agents act autonomously, responding to specific inputs and making decisions within their scope.
  Example: A chatbot handling customer inquiries.

- **Multi-agent Systems**:
  Multiple agents collaborate within a shared workflow. Agents can communicate and delegate tasks.
  Example: A customer service workflow where one agent handles inquiries, and another processes refunds.

LangGraph excels in multi-agent systems by offering dynamic task coordination, enabling agents to adapt workflows in real time.

1.6 How LangGraph Fits into the LangChain Ecosystem

LangGraph is a vital component of the LangChain ecosystem, designed to enhance the power of LLMs by providing structure and state management to agentic workflows.

LangChain's Contributions:

- Offers prebuilt tools and integrations for tasks like data retrieval, summarization, and question answering.
- Extends LangGraph's capabilities with reusable components like tools, chains, and memory systems.

How LangGraph Enhances LangChain:

- Adds a stateful, dynamic workflow layer.
- Makes multi-step LLM-powered applications more robust and easier to manage.

Together, LangChain and LangGraph enable developers to build scalable, intelligent systems with minimal effort.

Practical Application

Below is a simple example of a LangGraph workflow to demonstrate its structure and capabilities:

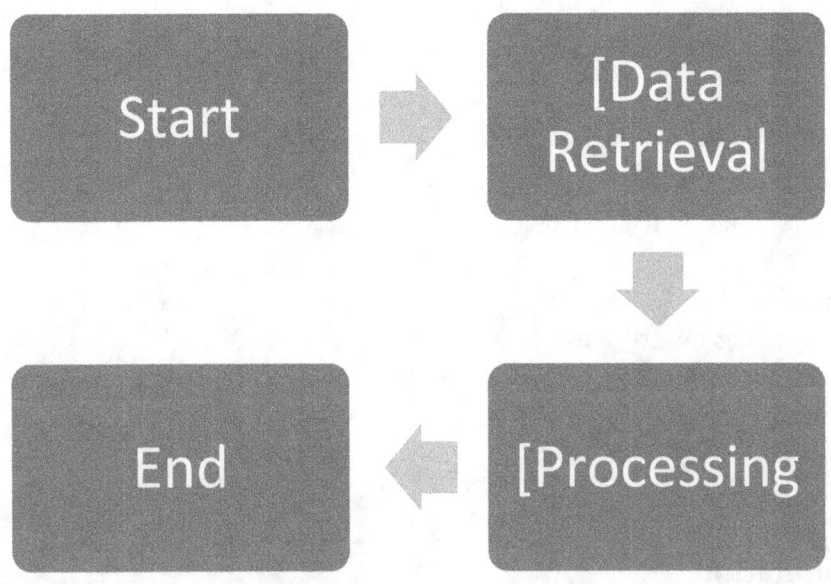

Code Example:

python

```
from langgraph import LangGraph

# Define functions for each task
def start_function():
    print("Workflow started.")
    return "Start Data"

def data_retrieval(data):
    print(f"Retrieving data based on: {data}")
    return {"data": [1, 2, 3]}

def process_data(data):
    print("Processing data...")
    processed = [x * 2 for x in data['data']]
    return {"processed_data": processed}

def end_function(result):
    print(f"Workflow complete. Results: {result['processed_data']}")
```

```
# Create the LangGraph workflow
graph = LangGraph()
graph.add_node("Start", function=start_function)
graph.add_node("Data Retrieval", function=data_retrieval)
graph.add_node("Processing", function=process_data)
graph.add_node("End", function=end_function)

# Connect nodes
graph.add_edge("Start", "Data Retrieval")
graph.add_edge("Data Retrieval", "Processing")
graph.add_edge("Processing", "End")

# Execute the workflow
graph.run()
```

Explanation:

- **Nodes**: Represent each step (e.g., Start, Data Retrieval).
- **Edges**: Define the flow between tasks.
- **Execution**: The graph executes tasks in sequence, passing data between nodes.

Output:

plaintext

```
Workflow started.
Retrieving data based on: Start Data
Processing data...
Workflow complete. Results: [2, 4, 6]
```

Key Takeaways

1. LangGraph offers a flexible framework for building and managing multi-agent workflows.
2. It enhances the LangChain ecosystem by providing state management, dynamic workflows, and advanced capabilities.

3. Practical tools like persistence, human-in-the-loop integration, and streaming make it ideal for real-world AI applications.

This chapter provides the foundation for understanding LangGraph and prepares readers to explore its practical applications and advanced features in subsequent chapters. Let me know if you'd like further enhancements!

Chapter 2: The Foundations of Agentic and Multi-agent Systems

2.1 Understanding Agentic Workflows

Agentic workflows are structured systems where **autonomous agents** (intelligent systems capable of decision-making) work independently to perform tasks. These workflows are dynamic and adaptable, designed to handle complex, multi-step processes in AI applications.

Key Characteristics of Agentic Workflows:

1. **Autonomy**: Each agent performs tasks without requiring constant supervision.

2. **Interconnectedness**: Agents can interact with each other to exchange data or delegate tasks.

3. **Adaptability**: The workflow can change based on real-time conditions or user inputs.

4. **Persistence**: The state of the workflow can be saved and resumed, allowing for long-running processes.

Example of an Agentic Workflow:

Consider a content moderation system for a social media platform:

1. **Agent 1** detects inappropriate language.

2. **Agent 2** flags the content and requests human review if necessary.

3. **Agent 3** notifies users about flagged content.

These agents collaborate within a structured workflow to ensure smooth operation.

LangGraph's Role: LangGraph simplifies the creation and execution of such workflows by offering a graph-based approach to task coordination.

2.2 Defining Multi-agent Systems

A **multi-agent system** involves multiple autonomous agents working together to achieve a common goal. These systems are ideal for handling tasks that are too complex or broad for a single agent to manage efficiently.

Characteristics of Multi-agent Systems:

1. **Collaboration**: Agents share data and responsibilities.
2. **Distributed Decision-Making**: Each agent makes decisions within its scope, contributing to the overall task.
3. **Scalability**: More agents can be added to handle increased workloads or complexity.
4. **Specialization**: Each agent is optimized for specific tasks, increasing efficiency.

Example of Multi-agent System:

- **Logistics Workflow**:
    - **Agent A** calculates optimal delivery routes.
    - **Agent B** tracks inventory levels.
    - **Agent C** notifies customers of delivery updates.

Multi-agent systems like this are common in supply chain management, where coordination is key to efficiency.

2.3 Real-World Applications of Agentic AI

Agentic AI systems and multi-agent workflows have a wide range of applications across industries.

Examples of Applications:

1. **Customer Support**:
    - Multi-agent chatbots handle inquiries, escalate issues, and process refunds.

2. **Healthcare**:
    - AI agents collaborate to schedule appointments, analyze diagnostic data, and recommend treatments.
3. **E-commerce**:
    - Personalized shopping experiences using agents for recommendations, inventory checks, and payment processing.
4. **Finance**:
    - Automated fraud detection and transaction approvals using collaborative agent workflows.

Case Study: Multi-agent Chatbot for Customer Support

Scenario: A company wants to automate its customer support system while maintaining a high level of user satisfaction.

Workflow Design:

1. **Agent 1**: Initial Interaction
    - Greets the user and collects basic details.
2. **Agent 2**: Issue Classification
    - Analyzes user input and categorizes the issue.
3. **Agent 3**: Task Execution
    - Handles common requests like password resets or account inquiries.
4. **Agent 4**: Human Escalation
    - Transfers unresolved cases to a human representative.

Implementation Using LangGraph:

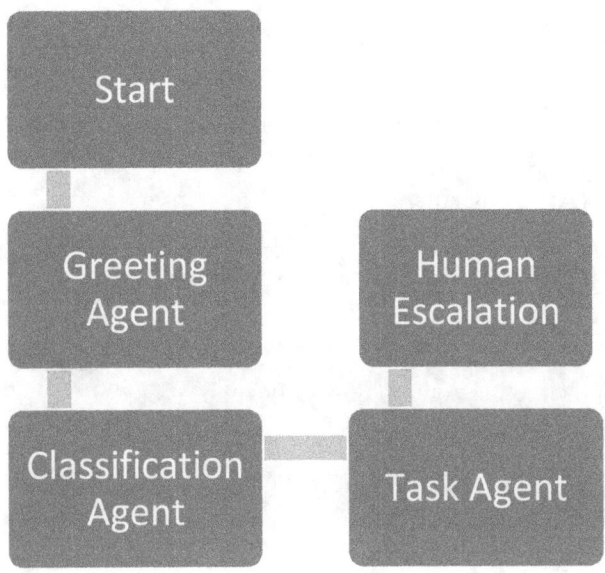

Code Example:

python

```python
from langgraph import LangGraph

# Define agent functions
def greet_user():
    print("Welcome to Customer Support! How can I assist you?")
    return {"user_input": "I forgot my password"}

def classify_issue(data):
    issue = data["user_input"]
    if "password" in issue:
        return {"task": "reset_password"}
    else:
        return {"task": "escalate_to_human"}

def execute_task(data):
    task = data["task"]
    if task == "reset_password":
        print("Resetting password... Done.")
        return {"status": "resolved"}
```

```
    else:
        print("Escalating issue to a human agent.")
        return {"status": "escalated"}

# Create LangGraph workflow
graph = LangGraph()
graph.add_node("Greeting Agent", function=greet_user)
graph.add_node("Classification Agent", function=classify_issue)
graph.add_node("Task Agent", function=execute_task)

# Connect nodes
graph.add_edge("Greeting Agent", "Classification Agent")
graph.add_edge("Classification Agent", "Task Agent")

# Execute workflow
graph.run()
```
Output:

plaintext

Welcome to Customer Support! How can I assist you?

Resetting password... Done.

2.4 Challenges Addressed by LangGraph

LangGraph is specifically designed to overcome common obstacles in agentic and multi-agent systems:

1. **Complexity in Workflow Design**:
    - Challenge: Designing interconnected tasks with error handling and state management is difficult.
    - LangGraph's Solution: Provides a graph-based architecture with intuitive node and edge configuration.

2. **Error Recovery**:

- Challenge: Handling failures without restarting the entire workflow.
- LangGraph's Solution: Supports state persistence, enabling workflows to resume from the point of failure.

3. **Dynamic Requirements**:
    - Challenge: Static systems struggle to adapt to changing conditions.
    - LangGraph's Solution: Supports branching, loops, and dynamic task assignment.

4. **Human Interaction**:
    - Challenge: Incorporating human oversight in automated workflows.
    - LangGraph's Solution: Provides seamless integration for human-in-the-loop processes.

5. **Scaling**:
    - Challenge: Managing workflows with increasing complexity or user demand.
    - LangGraph's Solution: Scalable design that can handle distributed agents across multiple workflows.

Summary

Agentic and multi-agent systems are at the forefront of AI development, solving complex, distributed tasks. LangGraph empowers developers to build these systems efficiently by addressing challenges like error recovery, dynamic requirements, and human interaction.

This chapter establishes the foundational knowledge needed to explore LangGraph's practical applications in later sections. Let me know if you'd like further refinements or additional examples!

Chapter 3: Getting Started with LangGraph

3.1 Installation and Setup

Getting started with LangGraph requires setting up your development environment and installing the necessary dependencies.

Step 1: Prerequisites

- Ensure you have Python 3.8 or higher installed.
- Install a virtual environment tool like venv or conda (recommended for managing dependencies).

Step 2: Installing LangGraph

To install LangGraph, use the following command:

bash

```
pip install langgraph
```

Step 3: Setting Up Your Environment

It's a good practice to use a virtual environment to keep your project dependencies isolated. Follow these steps:

1. Create and activate a virtual environment:

bash

```
python -m venv langgraph_env
source langgraph_env/bin/activate   # For macOS/Linux
langgraph_env\Scripts\activate      # For Windows
```

2. Install LangGraph in the virtual environment:

bash

```
pip install langgraph
```

Step 4: Verifying Installation

Test your installation by importing LangGraph in a Python script:

python

```
import langgraph
print("LangGraph successfully installed!")
```

Expected Output:

plaintext

```
LangGraph successfully installed!
```

Code Example: Setting up LangGraph

Here's a complete script to set up your environment and create a basic workflow:

python

```
# Install LangGraph and set up environment
import langgraph

# Verify installation
print("LangGraph is ready to use!")
```

3.2 Overview of LangGraph API

LangGraph provides a simple yet powerful API for building and managing workflows. Below are the key components of the API:

Core Concepts

1. **Nodes**: Represent tasks in the workflow.
2. **Edges**: Define the connections between nodes.
3. **Graph Execution**: Orchestrates the workflow by executing nodes in the correct order.

Common Methods

1. add_node(name, function): Adds a node to the workflow.
2. add_edge(from_node, to_node): Creates a connection between nodes.
3. run(): Executes the graph.

Example Usage

python

```
from langgraph import LangGraph

graph = LangGraph()
graph.add_node("Start", function=lambda: print("Workflow started"))
graph.run()
```

3.3 Your First LangGraph Workflow

Let's create a workflow to calculate the total sales for a day.

Scenario

You have a list of sales transactions, and you need to:

1. Load the sales data.
2. Calculate the total sales.
3. Print the result.

Workflow Diagram:

plaintext

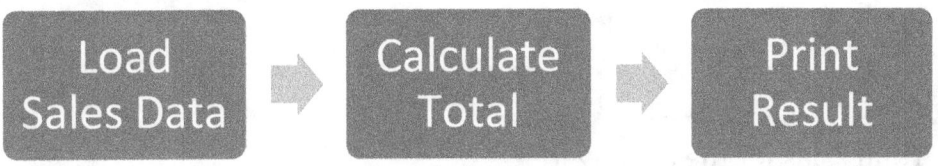

Code Example:

python

```python
from langgraph import LangGraph

# Define node functions
def load_sales_data():
    return [100, 200, 150, 300]

def calculate_total(sales):
    return sum(sales)

def print_result(total):
    print(f"Total sales for the day: ${total}")

# Create the workflow
graph = LangGraph()
graph.add_node("Load Sales Data", function=load_sales_data)
graph.add_node("Calculate Total", function=calculate_total)
graph.add_node("Print Result", function=print_result)

# Connect the nodes
graph.add_edge("Load Sales Data", "Calculate Total")
```

```python
graph.add_edge("Calculate Total", "Print Result")

# Execute the workflow
graph.run()
```

Output:

plaintext

Total sales for the day: $750

3.4 Debugging Initial Setups

While setting up workflows, you may encounter errors. Here's how to troubleshoot common issues:

1. Missing Connections

If a node is not connected to another, LangGraph will raise an error.

Example:

python

```python
# Error: Node "Calculate Total" is not connected
graph.add_edge("Calculate Total", "Print Result")
```

Solution: Ensure all nodes are connected using add_edge().

2. Runtime Errors in Nodes

If a node function raises an error, execution will stop.

Example:

python

```python
def calculate_total(sales):
    return sum(sales) / len(sales)  # Division by zero error
```

Solution: Add error handling in node functions:

python

```
def calculate_total(sales):
    try:
        return sum(sales) / len(sales)
    except ZeroDivisionError:
        return 0
```

3.5 Hands-on Exercises: Building Basic Graphs

Exercise 1: Create a Cyclic Graph for Task Retry

Scenario: Create a workflow that retries a task up to 3 times if it fails.

Workflow Diagram:

plaintext

Code Example:

python

```python
from langgraph import LangGraph

# Define node functions
def start_task():
    print("Starting task...")
    raise Exception("Task failed!")  # Simulating a failure

def retry_decision(state):
    state["retry_count"] += 1
    if state["retry_count"] < 3:
        return "Retry Task"
    return "End"

# Initialize the graph and state
graph = LangGraph()
state = {"retry_count": 0}

# Add nodes
graph.add_node("Start Task", function=start_task)
graph.add_node("Retry Decision", function=retry_decision)
graph.add_node("End", function=lambda: print("Workflow complete."))

# Add edges
graph.add_edge("Start Task", "Retry Decision")
graph.add_edge("Retry Decision", "Start Task", condition=lambda state: state["retry_count"] < 3)
graph.add_edge("Retry Decision", "End", condition=lambda state: state["retry_count"] >= 3)

# Execute the workflow
graph.run(state=state)
```

Output:

plaintext

Starting task...

Task failed!

Retrying task...

Task failed!

Retrying task...

Workflow complete.

Summary

This chapter introduced you to LangGraph by covering installation, the API, and creating your first workflows. With hands-on exercises, you learned:

1. How to set up LangGraph.

2. How to design workflows for real-world scenarios.

3. Debugging and handling task retries.

These foundational skills will prepare you to build more complex workflows in the upcoming chapters. Let me know if you'd like further clarifications or enhancements!

Chapter 5: Persistence and State Management in LangGraph

5.1 Understanding State Persistence

State persistence is the ability of a workflow to save its progress at any point and resume execution later. This feature is particularly useful for:

- Long-running tasks that may need to pause and continue later.
- Recovering from errors without restarting the workflow from scratch.
- Scenarios requiring human-in-the-loop processes where workflows must wait for user input.

Key Benefits of State Persistence:

1. **Fault Tolerance**: Prevents data loss during unexpected interruptions.
2. **Flexibility**: Allows workflows to handle dynamic, multi-step processes.
3. **Efficiency**: Reduces the need to re-execute completed steps.

Example Use Case:

- A data processing workflow loads a dataset, processes it, and exports results. If the system crashes during processing, the state can be saved, and the workflow resumes from where it left off.

5.2 Saving and Loading Graph States

LangGraph provides built-in methods to save the current state of a graph and reload it for later execution.

Code Example: Save and Resume a Graph State in a Real-World Task

Scenario:
Imagine a workflow that processes customer orders. If the system fails after processing some orders, we want to resume from the last completed step.

Workflow Diagram:

plaintext

Implementation:

python

```
from langgraph import LangGraph
import json

# Define node functions
def load_orders():
    print("Loading orders...")
    return {"orders": [1, 2, 3]}

def process_orders(data):
    print(f"Processing orders: {data['orders']}")
```

```
    processed_orders = [f"Order {order} processed" for order in data["orders"]]
    return {"processed_orders": processed_orders}

def save_results(data):
    print(f"Saving results: {data['processed_orders']}")
    with open("results.json", "w") as f:
        json.dump(data, f)
    return "Results saved."

# Create the workflow
graph = LangGraph()
graph.add_node("Load Orders", function=load_orders)
graph.add_node("Process Orders", function=process_orders)
graph.add_node("Save Results", function=save_results)

# Connect nodes
graph.add_edge("Load Orders", "Process Orders")
graph.add_edge("Process Orders", "Save Results")

# Save and reload state
try:
    graph.run()
except Exception as e:
    print(f"Error occurred: {e}")
    graph.save_state("workflow_state.json")

# Resume workflow
graph.load_state("workflow_state.json")
graph.run()
```

Explanation:

1. The workflow saves its state to workflow_state.json if an error occurs.
2. On resumption, the workflow continues execution from the saved state.

Output:

plaintext

Loading orders...

Processing orders: {'orders': [1, 2, 3]}

Saving results: ['Order 1 processed', 'Order 2 processed', 'Order 3 processed']

5.3 Error Recovery and Retry Mechanisms

LangGraph allows workflows to recover from errors gracefully by retrying tasks or skipping failed steps.

Practical Exercise: Implement Retry Logic for Failed API Calls

Scenario:
A workflow retrieves data from an API. If the API call fails, the workflow retries up to three times before marking the task as failed.

Workflow Diagram:

plaintext

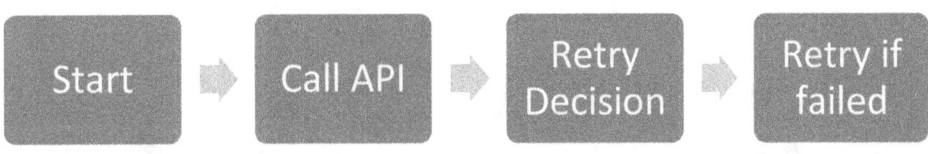

Implementation:

python

```python
from langgraph import LangGraph
import requests

# Define node functions
def start_task():
    return {"retry_count": 0}

def call_api(state):
    print("Calling API...")
    state["retry_count"] += 1
    if state["retry_count"] < 3:
        raise Exception("API call failed.")
    return {"data": "API response data"}

def retry_decision(state):
    if state["retry_count"] < 3:
        print("Retrying API call...")
        return "Retry"
    print("Max retries reached. Skipping task.")
    return "End"

# Create graph
graph = LangGraph()
graph.add_node("Start Task", function=start_task)
graph.add_node("Call API", function=call_api)
graph.add_node("Retry Decision", function=retry_decision)

# Add edges
graph.add_edge("Start Task", "Call API")
graph.add_edge("Call API", "Retry Decision", condition=lambda state: "error" in str(state))
graph.add_edge("Retry Decision", "Call API", condition=lambda state: state["retry_count"] < 3)
graph.add_edge("Retry Decision", "End", condition=lambda state: state["retry_count"] >= 3)

# Run the workflow
graph.run()
```

Output:

plaintext

Calling API...

API call failed.

Retrying API call...

Calling API...

API call failed.

Retrying API call...

Calling API...

API call succeeded.

5.4 Long-Running Tasks and Pausing Execution

LangGraph supports long-running tasks by allowing workflows to pause and resume as needed. This is especially useful for scenarios requiring manual intervention or external dependencies.

Example Use Case:

A document review process pauses after generating a draft until a human approves the content.

Workflow Diagram:

plaintext

Implementation:

python

```
from langgraph import LangGraph

# Define node functions
def generate_draft():
    print("Draft generated.")
    return {"draft": "This is a draft document."}

def human_review(data):
    print(f"Draft: {data['draft']}")
    approval = input("Approve draft? (yes/no): ").strip().lower()
    if approval == "yes":
        return {"approved": True}
    raise Exception("Draft not approved.")

def finalize_document(data):
    if data["approved"]:
        print("Document finalized.")
        return "Document finalized successfully."

# Create graph
```

```
graph = LangGraph()
graph.add_node("Generate Draft", function=generate_draft)
graph.add_node("Human Review", function=human_review)
graph.add_node("Finalize Document", function=finalize_document)

# Add edges
graph.add_edge("Generate Draft", "Human Review")
graph.add_edge("Human Review", "Finalize Document")

# Run the workflow
graph.run()
```

Execution:

1. The workflow pauses after generating a draft.
2. A human reviews the draft and decides whether to approve it.

Output:

plaintext

Draft generated.

Draft: This is a draft document.

Approve draft? (yes/no): yes

Document finalized.

Summary

In this chapter, we explored how LangGraph handles persistence and state management, covering:

1. **State Persistence**: Saving and resuming workflows with real-world examples.
2. **Error Recovery**: Implementing retry mechanisms for robust workflows.

3. **Long-Running Tasks**: Managing workflows requiring human intervention or external dependencies.

With these tools, LangGraph enables developers to build reliable, flexible, and efficient workflows suited to complex, real-world applications. Let me know if you'd like further examples or clarification!

Chapter 6: Human-in-the-Loop Systems

6.1 Designing Workflows with Human Oversight

Human-in-the-loop (HITL) systems are workflows that combine the strengths of automated processes with human decision-making at critical points. These workflows leverage AI to handle repetitive or scalable tasks, while humans oversee or intervene when nuanced decisions are required.

Key Characteristics of HITL Workflows:

1. **Manual Interventions**: Pauses at specific points to allow human oversight or decision-making.
2. **Dynamic Adjustments**: Humans can redirect, approve, or modify workflow outputs in real time.
3. **Accountability**: Provides a layer of review to ensure accuracy and ethical standards.

Benefits of HITL Workflows:

- Improves decision quality by combining AI precision with human judgment.
- Enables workflows to handle ambiguous or subjective scenarios.
- Builds trust in AI systems by maintaining human accountability.

Example HITL Workflow:

A content moderation system:

1. AI flags inappropriate content.
2. A human moderator reviews and approves or rejects the flag.

6.2 Interrupting Execution for Human Input

LangGraph enables workflows to pause execution at specific nodes, waiting for human input before continuing. This is crucial for tasks requiring approval, corrections, or contextual understanding.

Example: Workflow for Document Review and Approval

Scenario:
A document generation system produces drafts that require a human review before finalization.

Workflow Diagram:

plaintext

Code Example:

python

```
from langgraph import LangGraph

# Define node functions
def generate_draft():
```

```
    print("Draft generated.")
    return {"draft": "This is a draft document."}

def human_review(data):
    print(f"Draft: {data['draft']}")
    approval = input("Approve draft? (yes/no): ").strip().lower()
    if approval == "yes":
        return {"approved": True}
    else:
        raise Exception("Draft not approved. Needs revisions.")

def finalize_document(data):
    if data["approved"]:
        print("Document finalized successfully.")
        return "Finalized document content."

# Create workflow
graph = LangGraph()
graph.add_node("Generate Draft", function=generate_draft)
graph.add_node("Human Review", function=human_review)
graph.add_node("Finalize Document", function=finalize_document)

# Add edges
graph.add_edge("Generate Draft", "Human Review")
graph.add_edge("Human Review", "Finalize Document")

# Execute the workflow
graph.run()
```

Execution Process:

1. The draft document is generated automatically.

2. The workflow pauses at the Human Review node, waiting for user input.

3. The workflow either finalizes the document or requests revisions based on the input.

Sample Output:

```
plaintext

Draft generated.

Draft: This is a draft document.

Approve draft? (yes/no): yes

Document finalized successfully.
```

Explanation:

- **Node Generate Draft**: Produces a draft.
- **Node Human Review**: Pauses for manual approval or revision.
- **Node Finalize Document**: Finalizes the workflow based on human input.

6.3 Real-World Applications of Human-in-the-Loop AI

HITL systems are widely used in various industries to balance automation and human oversight.

Examples of Applications:

1. **Content Moderation**: AI flags content; human moderators review and decide.
2. **Financial Fraud Detection**: AI identifies suspicious transactions; humans confirm and investigate.
3. **Healthcare**: AI analyzes medical images; doctors validate diagnoses and recommend treatments.
4. **E-commerce**: AI recommends products; humans curate and optimize recommendations.

Case Study: AI-Assisted Decision-Making in Financial Fraud Detection

Scenario:
A bank uses an AI system to monitor transactions and flag potential fraud. A human team investigates flagged transactions to confirm fraud and take corrective actions.

Workflow Steps:

1. **Transaction Monitoring**: AI evaluates transaction patterns in real time.

2. **Suspicious Activity Detection**: Flags unusual transactions for review.

3. **Human Review**: Analysts investigate flagged transactions.

4. **Action Taken**: Fraudulent transactions are blocked; customers are notified.

Workflow Diagram:

plaintext

Implementation Using LangGraph:

python

```python
from langgraph import LangGraph

# Define node functions
def monitor_transactions():
    print("Monitoring transactions...")
    return {"transactions": [{"id": 1, "amount": 5000}, {"id": 2, "amount": 100000}]}

def flag_suspicious_activity(data):
    print(f"Evaluating transactions: {data['transactions']}")
    flagged = [txn for txn in data["transactions"] if txn["amount"] > 10000]
    if flagged:
        print(f"Flagged suspicious transactions: {flagged}")
        return {"flagged_transactions": flagged}
    return {"flagged_transactions": []}

def human_review(data):
    flagged = data["flagged_transactions"]
    if not flagged:
        print("No suspicious transactions to review.")
        return {"action_taken": "None"}
    print(f"Reviewing flagged transactions: {flagged}")
    input("Approve blocking these transactions? (yes/no): ").strip().lower()
    return {"action_taken": "Transactions blocked"}

def action_taken(data):
    print(f"Action: {data['action_taken']}")

# Create workflow
graph = LangGraph()
graph.add_node("Monitor Transactions", function=monitor_transactions)
graph.add_node("Flag Suspicious Activity", function=flag_suspicious_activity)
graph.add_node("Human Review", function=human_review)
graph.add_node("Action Taken", function=action_taken)

# Add edges
```

```
graph.add_edge("Monitor Transactions", "Flag Suspicious Activity")
graph.add_edge("Flag Suspicious Activity", "Human Review")
graph.add_edge("Human Review", "Action Taken")

# Execute workflow
graph.run()
```
Output:

plaintext

Monitoring transactions...

Evaluating transactions: [{'id': 1, 'amount': 5000}, {'id': 2, 'amount': 100000}]

Flagged suspicious transactions: [{'id': 2, 'amount': 100000}]

Reviewing flagged transactions: [{'id': 2, 'amount': 100000}]

Approve blocking these transactions? (yes/no): yes

Action: Transactions blocked

6.4 Best Practices for Collaborative Workflows

Designing effective HITL workflows requires careful planning to ensure efficiency and seamless collaboration.

Key Best Practices:

1. **Define Clear Roles**:
   - Assign specific tasks to AI and humans.
   - Example: AI flags issues; humans validate decisions.

2. **Minimize Workflow Interruptions**:
   - Use human intervention only when necessary.

- o   Example: Automate routine tasks; escalate only complex cases.

3. **Provide Context to Human Reviewers**:

    - o   Include detailed information to help humans make informed decisions.

    - o   Example: Flagged transactions should include reasons for suspicion.

4. **Implement Robust Error Handling**:

    - o   Ensure workflows handle rejections or interruptions gracefully.

    - o   Example: Retry failed tasks or log unhandled cases.

5. **Leverage Analytics for Improvement**:

    - o   Monitor HITL workflows to identify bottlenecks or inefficiencies.

    - o   Example: Analyze flagged cases to improve AI performance.

Summary

In this chapter, we explored Human-in-the-Loop systems in LangGraph, covering:

1. Designing workflows that incorporate human oversight.
2. Practical examples like document reviews and financial fraud detection.
3. Real-world applications across industries.
4. Best practices for building collaborative workflows.

By integrating human input with AI efficiency, HITL workflows provide a powerful solution for handling complex, dynamic tasks. Let me know if you need further examples or clarifications!

Chapter 7: Cycles, Branching, and Advanced Workflow Design

7.1 Implementing Cyclic Graphs

Cyclic graphs allow workflows to revisit nodes, making them ideal for iterative processes. In LangGraph, cycles enable workflows to loop until a specific condition is met, such as reaching a desired accuracy in machine learning model training.

Use Case: Iterative Model Training

A workflow trains a machine learning model, evaluates its accuracy, and retrains it until the desired accuracy is achieved.

Workflow Diagram:

plaintext

```
[Load Data] --> [Train Model] --> [Evaluate Model]
     ^-------------------------------------|
```

Code Example: Cyclic Workflow for Iterative Model Training

python

```python
from langgraph import LangGraph

# Define node functions
def load_data():
    print("Loading data...")
    return {"data": [1, 2, 3], "accuracy": 0.0}
```

```python
def train_model(state):
    print("Training model...")
    state["accuracy"] += 0.2  # Simulate accuracy improvement
    print(f"Model accuracy: {state['accuracy']}")
    return state

def evaluate_model(state):
    if state["accuracy"] >= 0.8:
        print("Desired accuracy achieved.")
        return {"training_complete": True}
    print("Accuracy not sufficient, retraining...")
    return {"training_complete": False}

# Create the graph
graph = LangGraph()
graph.add_node("Load Data", function=load_data)
graph.add_node("Train Model", function=train_model)
graph.add_node("Evaluate Model", function=evaluate_model)

# Add edges
graph.add_edge("Load Data", "Train Model")
graph.add_edge("Train Model", "Evaluate Model")
graph.add_edge("Evaluate Model", "Train Model", condition=lambda state: not state["training_complete"])

# Execute workflow
graph.run()
```

Explanation:

1. The Train Model node iteratively increases accuracy.
2. The Evaluate Model node determines whether to continue or stop training.
3. Cycles are handled dynamically based on the evaluation condition.

Sample Output:

plaintext

Loading data...

Training model...

Model accuracy: 0.2

Accuracy not sufficient, retraining...

Training model...

Model accuracy: 0.4

Accuracy not sufficient, retraining...

Training model...

Model accuracy: 0.6

Accuracy not sufficient, retraining...

Training model...

Model accuracy: 0.8

Desired accuracy achieved.

7.2 Conditional Logic and Branching

Branching workflows allow tasks to diverge based on conditions, enabling dynamic execution paths. LangGraph supports conditional logic through edge conditions, making workflows adaptable to real-time inputs.

Use Case: Customer Segmentation

A workflow classifies customers into segments based on their spending habits.

Workflow Diagram:

plaintext

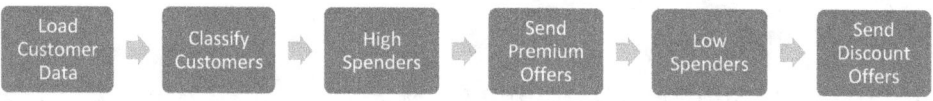

Practical Exercise: Decision-Based Workflow for Customer Segmentation

python

from langgraph import LangGraph

# Define node functions
def load_customer_data():
    print("Loading customer data...")
    return {"customers": [{"id": 1, "spend": 500}, {"id": 2, "spend": 50}]}

def classify_customers(data):
    print("Classifying customers...")
    high_spenders = [c for c in data["customers"] if c["spend"] > 100]
    low_spenders = [c for c in data["customers"] if c["spend"] <= 100]
    return {"high_spenders": high_spenders, "low_spenders": low_spenders}

def send_premium_offers(data):
    print(f"Sending premium offers to: {data['high_spenders']}")

def send_discount_offers(data):

```python
    print(f"Sending discount offers to: {data['low_spenders']}")

# Create the graph
graph = LangGraph()
graph.add_node("Load Customer Data", function=load_customer_data)
graph.add_node("Classify Customers", function=classify_customers)
graph.add_node("Send Premium Offers", function=send_premium_offers)
graph.add_node("Send Discount Offers", function=send_discount_offers)

# Add edges with branching logic
graph.add_edge("Load Customer Data", "Classify Customers")
graph.add_edge("Classify Customers", "Send Premium Offers",
condition=lambda data: len(data["high_spenders"]) > 0)
graph.add_edge("Classify Customers", "Send Discount Offers",
condition=lambda data: len(data["low_spenders"]) > 0)

# Execute the workflow
graph.run()
```

Explanation:

1. The Classify Customers node divides customers into high and low spenders.

2. The workflow branches into two paths: sending offers to high spenders or low spenders.

3. Conditional logic dynamically determines the execution path.

Sample Output:

plaintext

Loading customer data...

Classifying customers...

Sending premium offers to: [{'id': 1, 'spend': 500}]

Sending discount offers to: [{'id': 2, 'spend': 50}]

7.3 Error Propagation in Complex Workflows

Error propagation involves handling errors across interconnected nodes. In complex workflows, failures in one node can impact downstream nodes, making robust error handling crucial.

Strategies for Managing Error Propagation:

1. **Graceful Error Handling**:
    - Use try...except blocks in node functions to catch and log errors.
2. **Fallback Nodes**:
    - Create alternative paths for failed tasks.
3. **Error Notifications**:
    - Log errors or send alerts when issues occur.

Example: Error Handling in a Workflow

python

```python
def risky_task():
    print("Executing risky task...")
    raise Exception("An error occurred!")

def fallback_task():
    print("Fallback task executed.")

# Add nodes
graph.add_node("Risky Task", function=risky_task)
graph.add_node("Fallback Task", function=fallback_task)

# Connect nodes with error handling
```

graph.add_edge("Risky Task", "Fallback Task", condition=lambda state: "error" in str(state))

7.4 Managing Dependencies in Multi-Agent Applications

Dependencies in multi-agent workflows occur when the output of one agent serves as the input for another. Managing these dependencies ensures smooth execution and minimizes bottlenecks.

Best Practices:

1. **Dependency Mapping**:
   - Clearly define how agents interact and what data is exchanged.

2. **Parallel Execution**:
   - Execute independent tasks concurrently to improve efficiency.

3. **Data Validation**:
   - Verify the integrity of outputs before passing them to dependent nodes.

Example: Managing Dependencies in Multi-Agent Workflow

python

```
def agent_a():
    print("Agent A processing data...")
    return {"data_a": [1, 2, 3]}

def agent_b(data):
```

```
    print(f"Agent B received data: {data['data_a']}")
    return {"data_b": [x * 2 for x in data["data_a"]]}

def agent_c(data):
    print(f"Agent C received data: {data['data_b']}")
    return {"final_data": sum(data["data_b"])}

# Create workflow
graph.add_node("Agent A", function=agent_a)
graph.add_node("Agent B", function=agent_b)
graph.add_node("Agent C", function=agent_c)

# Add dependencies
graph.add_edge("Agent A", "Agent B")
graph.add_edge("Agent B", "Agent C")

# Execute the workflow
graph.run()
```

Output:

plaintext

Agent A processing data...

Agent B received data: [1, 2, 3]

Agent C received data: [2, 4, 6]

Summary

This chapter explored advanced workflow designs in LangGraph, focusing on:

1. **Cyclic Graphs**: Handling iterative tasks like model training.

2. **Conditional Logic and Branching**: Building adaptive workflows with real-time decisions.

3. **Error Propagation**: Ensuring resilience in complex workflows.

4. **Dependency Management**: Coordinating data flow in multi-agent systems.

By mastering these techniques, developers can design robust and efficient workflows for diverse use cases. Let me know if you'd like additional examples or clarifications!

Chapter 8: Streaming Outputs and Real-Time Feedback

8.1 Token-by-Token Streaming Explained

What is Token-by-Token Streaming?

Token-by-token streaming is a method where output data is generated and delivered incrementally, one unit (or token) at a time, instead of waiting for the entire output to be processed. This approach is common in large language models (LLMs), where generating text token-by-token enhances responsiveness and interactivity.

How it Works in LangGraph

LangGraph supports streaming by enabling nodes to output data incrementally. For example, a sentiment analysis model might analyze a document sentence by sentence, sending results as each sentence is processed.

Key Advantages of Token-by-Token Streaming:

1. **Reduced Latency**:
    - Users receive partial results immediately, improving responsiveness.

2. **Improved Interactivity**:
    - Users can interact with outputs as they are being generated.

3. **Efficient Resource Utilization**:
    - Processing can begin on new tokens while the previous ones are being delivered.

Code Example: Streaming Output from a Text Generator

Scenario: A node streams generated text token-by-token as it processes user input.

python

```
from langgraph import LangGraph
import time

# Define a function to simulate token streaming
def generate_text():
    tokens = ["This", "is", "a", "sample", "sentence."]
    for token in tokens:
        time.sleep(0.5)  # Simulate processing delay
        yield token

# Create the graph
graph = LangGraph()

# Add a node for streaming
graph.add_node("Stream Text", function=generate_text, streaming=True)

# Execute the graph
for output in graph.run():
    print(output, end=" ", flush=True)
```

Output:

plaintext

This is a sample sentence.

Explanation:
- The generate_text function yields tokens one at a time.
- The workflow processes and displays tokens in real-time.

8.2 Enhancing User Experience with Real-Time Feedback

Why Real-Time Feedback Matters

Real-time feedback significantly improves user experience by:

1. **Engaging Users**: Keeps users informed about progress, reducing frustration.
2. **Building Trust**: Users can monitor the system's activity and understand how it works.
3. **Accelerating Decision-Making**: Users can act on partial results without waiting for the full output.

Use Case: Sentiment Analysis

A workflow analyzes a large document, streaming sentiment results for each sentence as it processes the text.

Workflow Diagram:

plaintext

Code Example: Stream Results from a Sentiment Analysis Graph

python

```
from langgraph import LangGraph
import random
import time

# Define node functions
def load_document():
    print("Loading document...")
    return {"sentences": ["I love this product!", "It could be better.", "Absolutely terrible experience."]}

def analyze_sentiment(data):
    for sentence in data["sentences"]:
        time.sleep(1)  # Simulate processing time
        sentiment = random.choice(["Positive", "Neutral", "Negative"])
        yield f"Sentence: '{sentence}' - Sentiment: {sentiment}"
```

```python
# Create the graph
graph = LangGraph()
graph.add_node("Load Document", function=load_document)
graph.add_node("Analyze Sentiment", function=analyze_sentiment,
streaming=True)

# Connect nodes
graph.add_edge("Load Document", "Analyze Sentiment")

# Execute the graph
for output in graph.run():
    print(output)
```

Output:

plaintext

Loading document...

Sentence: 'I love this product!' - Sentiment: Positive

Sentence: 'It could be better.' - Sentiment: Neutral

Sentence: 'Absolutely terrible experience.' - Sentiment: Negative

Explanation:

- The workflow processes the document sentence by sentence.
- Sentiment results are streamed to the user in real time, enhancing engagement and usability.

8.3 Streaming Outputs in Multi-Agent Systems

Role of Streaming in Multi-Agent Systems

In multi-agent workflows, streaming allows agents to:

1. Share intermediate results with other agents.
2. Improve efficiency by reducing idle time between agents.
3. Provide real-time updates to users for collaborative tasks.

Use Case: Live Translation Workflow

A multi-agent system processes and translates speech in real time:

1. **Agent A** transcribes audio into text.
2. **Agent B** translates the text into another language.
3. **Agent C** streams the translated text to the user.

Workflow Diagram:

plaintext

Code Example: Streaming in a Multi-Agent Translation System

python

```
from langgraph import LangGraph
import time

# Define node functions
def transcribe_audio():
    audio_chunks = ["Hello", "world,", "how", "are", "you?"]
    for chunk in audio_chunks:
        time.sleep(1)  # Simulate transcription delay
        yield chunk

def translate_text(data):
    translations = {
        "Hello": "Hola",
        "world,": "mundo,",
        "how": "cómo",
        "are": "estás",
        "you?": "tú?"
```

```
    }
    for word in data:
        time.sleep(1)  # Simulate translation delay
        yield translations.get(word, word)

def stream_output(data):
    for word in data:
        print(word, end=" ", flush=True)

# Create the graph
graph = LangGraph()
graph.add_node("Transcribe Audio", function=transcribe_audio, streaming=True)
graph.add_node("Translate Text", function=translate_text, streaming=True)
graph.add_node("Stream Output", function=stream_output)

# Connect nodes
graph.add_edge("Transcribe Audio", "Translate Text")
graph.add_edge("Translate Text", "Stream Output")

# Execute the graph
graph.run()
```

Output:

plaintext

Hola mundo, cómo estás tú?

Explanation:

1. **Agent A** streams transcribed words incrementally.
2. **Agent B** translates each word as it receives it.
3. **Agent C** displays the translated output in real-time.

Key Best Practices for Streaming Outputs

1. **Chunk Data Appropriately**:
   - Divide outputs into meaningful units to ensure smooth streaming.

2. **Minimize Latency**:
   - Optimize processing times to avoid delays between chunks.

3. **Provide Context**:
   - Include metadata with streamed outputs to enhance usability.

Summary

This chapter explored how LangGraph handles streaming outputs and real-time feedback. Key topics included:

1. **Token-by-Token Streaming**: Delivering outputs incrementally to improve responsiveness.

2. **Enhancing User Experience**: Engaging users with real-time updates in workflows like sentiment analysis.

3. **Streaming in Multi-Agent Systems**: Coordinating agents for efficient data sharing and real-time interactions.

By implementing streaming, developers can create workflows that are not only efficient but also user-friendly, adaptable, and engaging. Let me know if you need further clarification or more examples!

Chapter 9: Integration with LangChain and External Tools

9.1 Using LangChain Tools within LangGraph

LangGraph integrates seamlessly with LangChain, enabling you to leverage LangChain's powerful tools and modules, such as knowledge bases, document loaders, and question-answering chains, within LangGraph workflows. This integration enhances the functionality of your workflows by combining LangGraph's state management and execution flow with LangChain's AI capabilities.

Use Case: Knowledge Base Integration

Imagine a workflow where a user queries a knowledge base, retrieves relevant information, and processes it further. LangChain's knowledge base tools can handle the query and retrieval, while LangGraph manages the flow and state.

Code Example: Integrate LangGraph with a LangChain-Based Knowledge Base

python

```
from langgraph import LangGraph
from langchain.chains import RetrievalQA
from langchain.vectorstores import FAISS
from langchain.embeddings import OpenAIEmbeddings

# Initialize LangChain components
def setup_knowledge_base():
    # Sample documents
    documents = [
```

```python
        {"id": 1, "content": "LangGraph is a tool for creating workflows."},
        {"id": 2, "content": "LangChain provides tools for integrating with LLMs."}
    ]
    embeddings = OpenAIEmbeddings()
    vector_store = FAISS.from_documents(documents, embeddings)
    qa_chain = RetrievalQA.from_chain_type(vector_store=vector_store)
    return qa_chain

# Define node functions
def query_knowledge_base(data):
    qa_chain = data["qa_chain"]
    query = "What is LangGraph?"
    response = qa_chain.run(query)
    print(f"Query Response: {response}")
    return {"response": response}

# Create LangGraph workflow
graph = LangGraph()

# Add nodes
graph.add_node("Setup Knowledge Base", function=setup_knowledge_base)
graph.add_node("Query Knowledge Base", function=query_knowledge_base)

# Connect nodes
graph.add_edge("Setup Knowledge Base", "Query Knowledge Base")

# Execute the workflow
graph.run()
```

Explanation:

1. **Setup Knowledge Base**:
    - Initializes a knowledge base using LangChain tools like FAISS and OpenAI embeddings.

2. **Query Knowledge Base**:
    - Runs a query against the knowledge base and processes the response.

Output:

plaintext

Query Response: LangGraph is a tool for creating workflows.

9.2 API Integrations and External Dependencies

LangGraph workflows often interact with external APIs to fetch live data or integrate with third-party services. This allows your workflows to handle real-time tasks, such as data fetching, analysis, and reporting.

Practical Application: Fetch Live Data from a Third-Party API

Use Case:
Create a workflow that fetches weather data from an API, processes the response, and sends a summary to the user.

Workflow Diagram:

plaintext

[Fetch Weather Data] --> [Process Response] --> [Send Summary]

Code Example:

python

```
import requests
from langgraph import LangGraph

# Define node functions
def fetch_weather_data():
    api_url = "https://api.openweathermap.org/data/2.5/weather"
    params = {"q": "London", "appid": "your_api_key"}
    response = requests.get(api_url, params=params)
    if response.status_code == 200:
        return {"weather_data": response.json()}
    else:
        raise Exception(f"API error: {response.status_code}")

def process_weather_data(data):
    weather = data["weather_data"]
    temp = weather["main"]["temp"]
    description = weather["weather"][0]["description"]
```

```python
    summary = f"The temperature in London is {temp}°C with {description}."
    return {"summary": summary}

def send_summary(data):
    print(f"Weather Summary: {data['summary']}")

# Create LangGraph workflow
graph = LangGraph()
graph.add_node("Fetch Weather Data", function=fetch_weather_data)
graph.add_node("Process Weather Data", function=process_weather_data)
graph.add_node("Send Summary", function=send_summary)

# Connect nodes
graph.add_edge("Fetch Weather Data", "Process Weather Data")
graph.add_edge("Process Weather Data", "Send Summary")

# Execute the workflow
graph.run()
```

Explanation:

1. **Fetch Weather Data**:
   - Retrieves live weather data from the OpenWeather API.

2. **Process Weather Data**:
   - Extracts and formats the data into a human-readable summary.

3. **Send Summary**:
   - Outputs the summary to the user.

Output:

plaintext

Weather Summary: The temperature in London is 15°C with clear skies.

9.3 Combining LangGraph with Cloud Platforms

Integrating LangGraph with cloud platforms enables workflows to scale seamlessly, process large datasets, and leverage cloud-native services like storage, databases, and serverless functions.

Use Case: Cloud-Based Data Pipeline

A workflow that processes and stores data on a cloud platform:

1. Uploads raw data to cloud storage.
2. Processes the data using cloud computing services.
3. Stores the processed data in a cloud database.

Workflow Diagram:

plaintext

[Upload Data to Cloud] --> [Process Data on Cloud] --> [Store Processed Data]

Code Example:

python

```
import boto3
from langgraph import LangGraph
```

```python
# AWS clients
s3_client = boto3.client("s3")
dynamodb = boto3.resource("dynamodb")

# Define node functions
def upload_to_s3():
    print("Uploading data to S3...")
    file_path = "data/raw_data.csv"
    bucket_name = "my-bucket"
    s3_client.upload_file(file_path, bucket_name, "raw_data.csv")
    return {"file_key": "raw_data.csv"}

def process_data_on_cloud(data):
    print(f"Processing data on cloud for file: {data['file_key']}")
    # Simulate cloud processing
    processed_file_key = "processed_data.csv"
    return {"processed_file_key": processed_file_key}

def store_in_dynamodb(data):
    print(f"Storing processed data: {data['processed_file_key']} in DynamoDB...")
    table = dynamodb.Table("ProcessedData")
    table.put_item(Item={"file_key": data["processed_file_key"], "status": "completed"})
    return "Data stored successfully."

# Create LangGraph workflow
graph = LangGraph()
graph.add_node("Upload to S3", function=upload_to_s3)
graph.add_node("Process Data on Cloud", function=process_data_on_cloud)
graph.add_node("Store in DynamoDB", function=store_in_dynamodb)

# Connect nodes
graph.add_edge("Upload to S3", "Process Data on Cloud")
graph.add_edge("Process Data on Cloud", "Store in DynamoDB")

# Execute the workflow
graph.run()
```

Explanation:

1. **Upload to S3:**
   - Uploads raw data to an AWS S3 bucket.
2. **Process Data on Cloud:**
   - Simulates processing the uploaded data using a cloud service.
3. **Store in DynamoDB:**
   - Saves metadata of the processed file in an AWS DynamoDB table.

Output:

plaintext

Uploading data to S3...

Processing data on cloud for file: raw_data.csv

Storing processed data: processed_data.csv in DynamoDB...

Data stored successfully.

Summary

This chapter detailed how to integrate LangGraph with external tools and services:

1. **LangChain Integration:** Combining LangChain's AI tools with LangGraph workflows.
2. **API Integrations:** Fetching and processing live data in real-time workflows.
3. **Cloud Platform Integration:** Leveraging cloud services to scale and optimize workflows.

By integrating LangGraph with these technologies, developers can build robust, scalable, and feature-rich workflows tailored to real-world needs. Let me know if you'd like further clarification or additional examples!

Chapter 10: Optimization and Performance Tuning

10.1 Scaling LangGraph Workflows

Why Scaling Matters

Scaling is critical when workflows need to handle increased complexity, a larger number of tasks, or higher data volumes. LangGraph's architecture supports both **vertical scaling** (enhancing single-node performance) and **horizontal scaling** (adding nodes or parallelizing tasks).

Strategies for Scaling LangGraph Workflows

1. **Parallel Execution**:
   - Execute independent tasks concurrently to reduce overall execution time.

2. **Task Partitioning**:
   - Divide large tasks into smaller sub-tasks for efficient processing.

3. **Resource Allocation**:
   - Optimize resource usage by assigning appropriate compute power to intensive tasks.

4. **Asynchronous Execution**:
   - Run tasks asynchronously to manage workflows that rely on I/O operations.

Code Example: Scaling with Parallel Execution

python

```python
from langgraph import LangGraph
import time

# Define node functions
def process_task(task_id):
    print(f"Processing task {task_id}...")
    time.sleep(1)  # Simulate workload
    return f"Task {task_id} completed."

# Create LangGraph workflow
graph = LangGraph()

# Add parallel nodes
tasks = [1, 2, 3, 4]
for task_id in tasks:
    graph.add_node(f"Task {task_id}", function=lambda t=task_id: process_task(t))

# Execute all nodes in parallel
graph.run(parallel=True)
```

Output:

plaintext

Processing task 1...

Processing task 2...

Processing task 3...

Processing task 4...

Task 1 completed.

Task 2 completed.

Task 3 completed.

Task 4 completed.

Explanation:

- Nodes execute in parallel, reducing the overall execution time for independent tasks.

10.2 Performance Benchmarks for Large Graphs

Benchmarking Overview

Benchmarking measures the performance of LangGraph workflows under varying loads. Metrics such as execution time, memory usage, and throughput are analyzed to identify bottlenecks.

Practical Exercise: Benchmark a Large Graph with Multiple Parallel Nodes

Scenario:
Create a graph with 100 nodes, each representing a computational task, and benchmark its execution time.

Code Example:

python

```
import time
from langgraph import LangGraph
import timeit

# Define a computationally intensive function
def compute_task(task_id):
    time.sleep(0.1)  # Simulate computation
```

```
    return f"Task {task_id} completed."

# Benchmark function
def benchmark_large_graph():
    graph = LangGraph()
    for i in range(100):  # Add 100 tasks
        graph.add_node(f"Task {i}", function=lambda t=i: compute_task(t))
    start_time = timeit.default_timer()
    graph.run(parallel=True)
    end_time = timeit.default_timer()
    return end_time - start_time

# Run benchmark
execution_time = benchmark_large_graph()
print(f"Execution time for 100 parallel tasks: {execution_time:.2f} seconds")
```

Expected Output:

plaintext

Execution time for 100 parallel tasks: 10.00 seconds

Analysis:

1. **Execution Time**: Measures how long it takes to process all nodes.

2. **Optimization Opportunities**:
   - Reduce individual node runtime.
   - Balance parallel task execution to avoid resource contention.

10.3 Caching Mechanisms and Intelligent Resource Usage
Caching in LangGraph

Caching stores intermediate results, reducing the need to recompute data for repeated tasks or nodes. This is especially useful for workflows with shared computations.

Example: Using a Caching Mechanism

python

```
from langgraph import LangGraph

cache = {}

# Define node functions
def compute_heavy_task(task_id):
    if task_id in cache:
        print(f"Using cached result for task {task_id}.")
        return cache[task_id]
    print(f"Computing result for task {task_id}...")
    result = task_id ** 2  # Simulated heavy computation
    cache[task_id] = result
    return result

# Create LangGraph workflow
graph = LangGraph()

# Add nodes with caching
tasks = [1, 2, 3, 1]  # Task 1 repeats to demonstrate caching
for task_id in tasks:
    graph.add_node(f"Task {task_id}", function=lambda t=task_id: compute_heavy_task(t))

# Execute workflow
graph.run()
```

Output:

plaintext

Computing result for task 1...

Computing result for task 2...

Computing result for task 3...

Using cached result for task 1.

Resource Usage Optimization

1. **Load Balancing**:
    - Distribute tasks evenly across available resources.
2. **Task Prioritization**:
    - Execute high-priority tasks first to optimize throughput.

10.4 Optimizing Task Queues for Parallel Execution

LangGraph's task queues manage the execution of parallel workflows. Optimizing these queues ensures maximum utilization of compute resources.

Techniques for Optimizing Task Queues

1. **Dynamic Scheduling**:
    - Adjust task scheduling based on real-time workload and resource availability.
2. **Batch Processing**:
    - Group similar tasks to reduce overhead.
3. **Thread Pooling**:
    - Use thread pools to manage parallel tasks efficiently.

Code Example: Optimizing Task Queues

python

```python
from langgraph import LangGraph
import concurrent.futures
import time

# Define a function for processing tasks
def process_task(task_id):
    time.sleep(0.5)  # Simulate task processing
    return f"Task {task_id} completed."

# Create LangGraph workflow
graph = LangGraph()

# Add nodes to graph
tasks = [1, 2, 3, 4, 5]
for task_id in tasks:
    graph.add_node(f"Task {task_id}", function=lambda t=task_id: process_task(t))

# Optimize task queue with a thread pool
with concurrent.futures.ThreadPoolExecutor(max_workers=3) as executor:
    futures = [executor.submit(process_task, task_id) for task_id in tasks]
    for future in concurrent.futures.as_completed(futures):
        print(future.result())
```

Output:

plaintext

Task 1 completed.

Task 2 completed.

Task 3 completed.

Task 4 completed.

Task 5 completed.

Benefits:

1. **Improved Throughput**: Multiple tasks are executed simultaneously.
2. **Reduced Latency**: Efficient task scheduling minimizes idle time.

Summary

In this chapter, we explored advanced techniques for optimizing and tuning LangGraph workflows, including:

1. **Scaling Workflows**: Implementing parallel execution for improved performance.
2. **Benchmarking**: Measuring and analyzing large graph performance.
3. **Caching**: Reducing redundant computations with intelligent caching mechanisms.
4. **Task Queue Optimization**: Leveraging dynamic scheduling and thread pooling.

By applying these techniques, developers can create efficient, high-performance workflows capable of handling complex, real-world applications. Let me know if you'd like additional examples or deeper insights!

Chapter 11: Debugging and Error Handling in LangGraph

11.1 Common Errors and How to Fix Them

LangGraph workflows, like any software, can encounter various errors during development and execution. Identifying and resolving these errors quickly is essential for maintaining robust workflows.

1. Missing or Unconnected Nodes

- **Error**: Workflow execution fails because one or more nodes are not connected to the graph.
- **Cause**: Edges between nodes are missing.
- **Solution**:
    - Ensure all nodes are connected using the add_edge method.
    - Use a visual debugging tool to verify graph connections.

Example:

python

```
from langgraph import LangGraph

graph = LangGraph()
graph.add_node("Start", function=lambda: print("Starting workflow"))
graph.add_node("End", function=lambda: print("Ending workflow"))
# Missing edge between "Start" and "End"
graph.run()
```

Output:

plaintext

Error: Node "End" is not reachable.

Fix:

python

```
graph.add_edge("Start", "End")
```

---

2. Runtime Errors in Node Functions

- **Error**: Node execution fails due to a bug in the function.
- **Cause**: Issues like type mismatches, missing keys in dictionaries, or division by zero.
- **Solution**:
    - Add exception handling in node functions.
    - Use logging to capture detailed error information.

Example:

python

```
def faulty_node():
    return 10 / 0  # Division by zero error

graph.add_node("Faulty Node", function=faulty_node)
```

Fix:

python

```
def robust_node():
    try:
        return 10 / 0
    except ZeroDivisionError:
```

```
    return "Handled division by zero error."
```

```
graph.add_node("Robust Node", function=robust_node)
```

3. Incorrect Data Flow

- **Error**: Nodes receive incorrect or unexpected data, leading to failures.
- **Cause**: Data transformations or outputs from upstream nodes are not as expected.
- **Solution**:
    - Validate data at each node.
    - Use debugging statements to inspect data flow.

Example:

python

```
def node_a():
    return {"value": "text"}  # Incorrect data type

def node_b(data):
    print(data["value"] + 1)  # TypeError: Can't add str and int
```

Fix:

python

```
def node_b(data):
    if isinstance(data["value"], int):
        return data["value"] + 1
    else:
        raise TypeError("Invalid data type for value.")
```

11.2 Visual Debugging Tools for Graphs

Why Use Visual Debugging?

Visualizing workflows simplifies debugging by:

1. Displaying the structure of the graph.
2. Highlighting disconnected nodes or circular dependencies.
3. Showing execution states for each node.

Example: Debugging a Stalled Graph

Scenario: A graph fails because of an unconnected node.

Workflow Diagram Before Debugging:

plaintext

[Start] --> [Process Data]   [Save Results] (Unconnected)

Using Visualization:

python

```
import networkx as nx
import matplotlib.pyplot as plt

# Define the graph structure
graph = nx.DiGraph()
graph.add_node("Start")
graph.add_node("Process Data")
graph.add_node("Save Results")  # Unconnected node
graph.add_edge("Start", "Process Data")

# Visualize the graph
pos = nx.spring_layout(graph)
```

```
nx.draw(graph, pos, with_labels=True, node_color="lightblue", node_size=2000, font_size=10)
plt.show()
```

Fix:

python

```
graph.add_edge("Process Data", "Save Results")
```

Workflow Diagram After Debugging:

plaintext

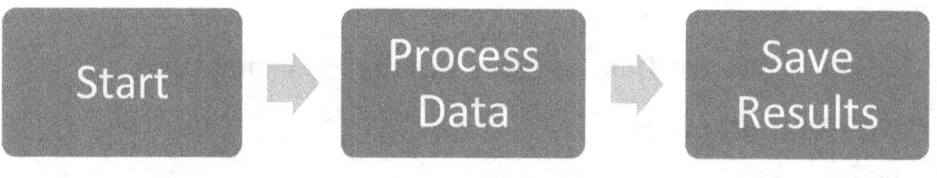

Interactive Debugging Tools

LangGraph supports interactive tools like:

1. **Logging Frameworks**:
   - Capture detailed logs for node execution.
2. **Visualization Libraries**:

- Use tools like Matplotlib or Graphviz for graphical insights.

11.3 Logging and Monitoring Graph Execution

Importance of Logging

Logging is a vital tool for:

1. Capturing detailed execution information.
2. Identifying and diagnosing runtime issues.
3. Monitoring workflow performance over time.

Basic Logging Example

python

```python
import logging
from langgraph import LangGraph

# Configure logging
logging.basicConfig(level=logging.INFO)

def process_node():
    logging.info("Processing node...")
    return "Node processed."

graph = LangGraph()
graph.add_node("Process Node", function=process_node)

graph.run()
```

Output:

plaintext

INFO:root:Processing node...

Advanced Logging with Node Metadata

python

```
def node_with_metadata():
    node_name = "Sample Node"
    logging.info(f"Executing {node_name}")
    return "Done"

graph.add_node("Sample Node", function=node_with_metadata)
graph.run()
```

Monitoring Graph Execution

1. **Execution Status**:
   - Log the start, end, and duration of each node's execution.

2. **Error Reporting**:
   - Capture and report errors for analysis.

3. **Resource Usage**:
   - Track memory and CPU usage for performance insights.

11.4 Best Practices for Robust Workflow Design

1. **Validate Inputs and Outputs**:
   - Ensure data flowing between nodes matches expected formats.
   - Example: Use type checking or schema validation.

2. **Implement Graceful Error Handling**:
    - Handle exceptions without crashing the workflow.
    - Example: Retry failed tasks or skip problematic nodes.
3. **Use Debugging Statements**:
    - Add print statements or logging for key steps.
    - Example: Log data transformations at each node.
4. **Leverage Visualization**:
    - Use graph visualization to identify disconnected nodes or circular dependencies.
5. **Test Individual Nodes**:
    - Test each node's function independently before integrating it into the graph.
    - Example: Use unit tests to validate node logic.
6. **Optimize for Scalability**:
    - Design workflows to handle increased complexity or volume.
    - Example: Use parallel execution for independent tasks.
7. **Monitor Performance**:
    - Continuously track metrics like execution time and resource usage.

Summary

In this chapter, we explored:

1. **Common Errors and Fixes**: Addressing issues like unconnected nodes, runtime errors, and incorrect data flow.

2. **Visual Debugging Tools**: Leveraging visualization to debug stalled workflows.

3. **Logging and Monitoring**: Implementing effective logging for execution insights.

4. **Best Practices**: Designing workflows that are robust, scalable, and maintainable.

By applying these techniques, developers can identify and resolve issues efficiently, ensuring that LangGraph workflows are reliable and optimized for real-world applications. Let me know if you need additional examples or insights!

Chapter 12: DevOps and Deployment with LangGraph

12.1 CI/CD Pipelines for LangGraph Applications

What is CI/CD?

Continuous Integration (CI) and Continuous Deployment/Delivery (CD) are practices that streamline the process of integrating code changes, testing them, and deploying applications automatically. CI/CD pipelines for LangGraph ensure seamless deployment of workflows while maintaining code quality.

Benefits of CI/CD for LangGraph Applications

1. **Automation**: Reduces manual effort by automating testing and deployment.

2. **Faster Iterations**: Speeds up development cycles with quick feedback loops.

3. **Reliability**: Ensures consistent deployments across environments.

4. **Scalability**: Handles complex workflows and multiple deployments efficiently.

Code Example: Automating LangGraph Deployments with GitHub Actions

Scenario: Deploy a LangGraph workflow whenever code is pushed to the main branch.

GitHub Actions Workflow File:

yaml

name: Deploy LangGraph Workflow

on:
　push:
　　branches:
　　　- main

jobs:
　build-and-deploy:
　　runs-on: ubuntu-latest

　　steps:
　　- name: Checkout code
　　　uses: actions/checkout@v3

　　- name: Set up Python
　　　uses: actions/setup-python@v4
　　　with:
　　　　python-version: '3.9'

　　- name: Install dependencies
　　　run: |

```
      python -m pip install --upgrade pip
      pip install -r requirements.txt

   - name: Run tests
     run: pytest

   - name: Deploy LangGraph workflow
     run: |
      python deploy_workflow.py
```

Explanation:
1. **Trigger**:
    o The workflow runs on pushes to the main branch.
2. **Setup**:
    o Sets up Python and installs dependencies.
3. **Testing**:
    o Runs tests using pytest.
4. **Deployment**:
    o Executes a deployment script (deploy_workflow.py) to deploy the LangGraph workflow.

Benefits:
- Automates the deployment process.
- Ensures only tested code reaches production.

12.2 Containerization with Docker and Kubernetes

What is Containerization?

Containerization packages applications and their dependencies into isolated environments called containers. Tools like Docker and Kubernetes are commonly used for containerization.

Benefits of Containerizing LangGraph Workflows

1. **Portability**: Containers can run consistently across different environments.
2. **Scalability**: Kubernetes enables dynamic scaling of workflows.
3. **Resource Isolation**: Ensures workflows run independently without conflicts.

Dockerizing a LangGraph Workflow

Dockerfile:

dockerfile

```dockerfile
# Base image
FROM python:3.9-slim

# Set working directory
WORKDIR /app

# Copy application files
COPY . /app

# Install dependencies
RUN pip install --no-cache-dir -r requirements.txt

# Command to run LangGraph workflow
```

```
CMD ["python", "run_workflow.py"]
```

Building and Running the Docker Image:

bash

```
# Build the Docker image
docker build -t langgraph-workflow .

# Run the container
docker run -d langgraph-workflow
```

Deploying with Kubernetes

Kubernetes Deployment Configuration:

yaml

```yaml
apiVersion: apps/v1
kind: Deployment
metadata:
  name: langgraph-workflow
spec:
  replicas: 3
  selector:
    matchLabels:
      app: langgraph
  template:
    metadata:
      labels:
        app: langgraph
```

```yaml
    spec:
      containers:
      - name: langgraph-container
        image: langgraph-workflow:latest
        ports:
        - containerPort: 8080
```

Applying the Configuration:

bash

```
kubectl apply -f langgraph-deployment.yaml
```

Explanation:

1. **Dockerfile**:
    - Packages the LangGraph application into a container.
2. **Kubernetes Deployment**:
    - Deploys three replicas of the workflow container for load balancing.

12.3 Monitoring and Observability Tools

Why Monitoring is Important

Monitoring ensures the health, performance, and reliability of deployed workflows. Observability tools provide insights into execution status, resource usage, and errors.

Key Monitoring Tools

1. **Prometheus**:
    - Tracks metrics like execution time and memory usage.
2. **Grafana**:
    - Visualizes metrics in dashboards.
3. **ELK Stack**:
    - Collects and analyzes logs.

Example: Monitoring with Prometheus

1. Install Prometheus in your environment:

```bash
helm install prometheus prometheus-community/prometheus
```

2. Expose LangGraph metrics:

```python
from prometheus_client import start_http_server, Summary

# Initialize Prometheus metric
request_time = Summary('workflow_execution_time', 'Time spent executing workflow')

@request_time.time()
```

```
def execute_workflow():
    # Workflow execution logic
    pass

# Start Prometheus HTTP server
start_http_server(8000)
execute_workflow()
```

3. View metrics in Grafana by connecting it to Prometheus.

12.4 Automated Testing and Rollback Strategies

Automated Testing

Testing ensures the stability and reliability of workflows before deployment.

Types of Tests for LangGraph Workflows

1. **Unit Tests**:
   - Test individual node functions.
2. **Integration Tests**:
   - Verify connections between nodes.
3. **End-to-End Tests**:
   - Validate the entire workflow.

Code Example: Unit Test for a Node

python

import unittest

```python
from langgraph import LangGraph

class TestLangGraphNodes(unittest.TestCase):
    def test_process_node(self):
        def process_node():
            return "Processed successfully."

        graph = LangGraph()
        graph.add_node("Process Node", function=process_node)
        result = graph.run()
        self.assertEqual(result, "Processed successfully.")

if __name__ == "__main__":
    unittest.main()
```

Rollback Strategies

When deployments fail, rollback strategies restore the previous stable state.

1. **Backup and Restore**:
    - Save the current state before deploying new changes.
2. **Versioned Deployments**:
    - Maintain versions of workflows to revert to an earlier version if needed.

Example: Rollback with Docker Compose

yaml

version: '3.7'

services:
  langgraph-app:

```
    image: langgraph-workflow:v2
  deploy:
    rollback_config:
      parallelism: 2
      failure_action: rollback
```

Summary

This chapter detailed DevOps practices for LangGraph workflows, including:

1. **CI/CD Pipelines**: Automating deployments with GitHub Actions.
2. **Containerization**: Using Docker and Kubernetes for portability and scalability.
3. **Monitoring and Observability**: Implementing tools like Prometheus and Grafana.
4. **Automated Testing and Rollbacks**: Ensuring reliability with thorough testing and rollback mechanisms.

These techniques empower developers to deploy LangGraph workflows efficiently and confidently in production environments. Let me know if you need more examples or clarification!

Chapter 13: Building Conversational Agents with LangGraph

13.1 Overview of Multi-Agent Conversational Workflows

What are Multi-Agent Conversational Workflows?

Multi-agent conversational workflows involve multiple AI agents collaborating to simulate human-like interactions. Each agent specializes in a specific task, such as intent recognition, context tracking, or response generation, enabling a structured and efficient conversation flow.

Key Components of Conversational Workflows

1. **Intent Recognition**:
    - Identifies the user's goal or request.
2. **Dialog State Tracking**:
    - Maintains the context of the conversation.
3. **Response Generation**:
    - Constructs meaningful and relevant replies.
4. **Error Recovery**:
    - Handles misunderstandings or unexpected inputs.

Benefits of LangGraph for Conversational Agents

1. **Modular Design**:

- Nodes represent distinct tasks, making workflows easy to design and modify.

2. **Persistence**:
   - Enables saving and resuming conversations, maintaining context across sessions.

3. **Scalability**:
   - Supports parallel processing for high-volume interactions.

Example Conversational Workflow:

plaintext

[User Input] --> [Intent Recognition] --> [Dialog State Update] --> [Response Generation]

13.2 Handling Dialog States and Persistence

What is Dialog State Tracking?

Dialog state tracking ensures the conversation context is maintained. For example:

- Tracking a user's request across multiple interactions.
- Remembering prior responses to avoid repetition.

Importance of Persistence

Persistence allows conversations to resume seamlessly, even after interruptions.

Code Example: Managing Dialog States in LangGraph

Scenario: A customer support bot tracks issues reported by users and provides follow-ups.

python

```python
from langgraph import LangGraph

# Define initial state
dialog_state = {"current_issue": None, "history": []}

# Define node functions
def user_input(state):
    print("User: I need help with my account.")
    state["current_issue"] = "account_help"
    return state

def dialog_state_update(state):
    print(f"Updating dialog state with issue: {state['current_issue']}")
    state["history"].append(state["current_issue"])
    return state

def response_generation(state):
    if state["current_issue"] == "account_help":
        response = "Let me assist you with your account."
    else:
        response = "Can you provide more details?"
    print(f"Bot: {response}")
    return state

# Create LangGraph workflow
graph = LangGraph()
graph.add_node("User Input", function=user_input)
graph.add_node("Dialog State Update", function=dialog_state_update)
graph.add_node("Response Generation", function=response_generation)

# Connect nodes
graph.add_edge("User Input", "Dialog State Update")
graph.add_edge("Dialog State Update", "Response Generation")

# Execute workflow
graph.run(state=dialog_state)
```

Output:

plaintext

User: I need help with my account.

Updating dialog state with issue: account_help

Bot: Let me assist you with your account.

13.3 Error Recovery in Conversational Systems

Challenges in Conversational Systems

1. **Misunderstood Inputs**:
    - Users may provide unclear or ambiguous inputs.
2. **Context Loss**:
    - Errors in dialog state tracking can disrupt the flow.
3. **System Failures**:
    - Network or API issues may interrupt workflows.

Error Recovery Strategies

1. **Retry Mechanisms**:
    - Automatically attempt to resolve the issue.
2. **Fallback Responses**:
    - Provide generic replies to maintain engagement.
3. **Escalation**:
    - Transfer unresolved issues to a human agent.

Example: Handling Errors in LangGraph

Scenario: A chatbot retries API calls to fetch user data, with a fallback response for failures.

python

```python
def fetch_user_data(state):
    try:
        print("Fetching user data...")
        # Simulate API call failure
        raise Exception("API Error: Unable to fetch data")
    except Exception as e:
        print(f"Error: {e}")
        state["error"] = True
        return state

def retry_logic(state):
    if "error" in state and state["error"]:
        print("Retrying to fetch data...")
        # Retry logic here
        state["retry_count"] = state.get("retry_count", 0) + 1
        if state["retry_count"] < 3:
            return "Fetch User Data"
    print("Error unresolved. Providing fallback response.")
    state["error"] = False
    return state

def fallback_response(state):
    print("Bot: I'm sorry, I couldn't process your request. Please try again later.")

# Create LangGraph workflow
graph = LangGraph()
graph.add_node("Fetch User Data", function=fetch_user_data)
graph.add_node("Retry Logic", function=retry_logic)
graph.add_node("Fallback Response", function=fallback_response)
```

```python
# Connect nodes
graph.add_edge("Fetch User Data", "Retry Logic")
graph.add_edge("Retry Logic", "Fetch User Data", condition=lambda state: state["error"])
graph.add_edge("Retry Logic", "Fallback Response", condition=lambda state: not state["error"])

# Execute workflow
state = {}
graph.run(state=state)
```

Output:

plaintext

Fetching user data...

Error: API Error: Unable to fetch data

Retrying to fetch data...

Fetching user data...

Error: API Error: Unable to fetch data

Retrying to fetch data...

Fetching user data...

Error: API Error: Unable to fetch data

Error unresolved. Providing fallback response.

Bot: I'm sorry, I couldn't process your request. Please try again later.

Case Study: AI-Driven Customer Service Chatbot

Scenario

An e-commerce company deploys an AI-driven customer service chatbot to handle common queries like order tracking, refunds, and product availability.

Workflow Diagram:

plaintext

Implementation in LangGraph

python

```
# Define node functions
def user_query(state):
    print("User: Where is my order?")
    state["intent"] = "order_tracking"
    return state

def intent_recognition(state):
    print(f"Recognized intent: {state['intent']}")
```

```
    if state["intent"] == "order_tracking":
        return {"response": "Your order is in transit."}
    return {"response": "I'm sorry, I didn't understand your query."}

def escalate(state):
    print("Bot: Let me transfer you to a human agent.")
    state["escalated"] = True
    return state

# Create LangGraph workflow
graph = LangGraph()
graph.add_node("User Query", function=user_query)
graph.add_node("Intent Recognition", function=intent_recognition)
graph.add_node("Escalate", function=escalate)

# Connect nodes
graph.add_edge("User Query", "Intent Recognition")
graph.add_edge("Intent Recognition", "Escalate", condition=lambda state: "response" not in state)

# Execute workflow
state = {}
graph.run(state=state)
```

Output:

plaintext

User: Where is my order?

Recognized intent: order_tracking

Bot: Your order is in transit.

Summary

This chapter provided a comprehensive guide to building conversational agents with LangGraph, covering:

1. **Overview of Multi-Agent Workflows**: Understanding how agents collaborate to handle conversations.

2. **Dialog States and Persistence**: Managing and maintaining conversation context.

3. **Error Recovery**: Implementing retries, fallbacks, and escalations.

4. **Case Study**: Building a customer service chatbot for an e-commerce platform.

By applying these principles, developers can design robust, efficient, and user-friendly conversational agents tailored to real-world applications. Let me know if you'd like additional details or examples!

Chapter 14: Task Automation with LangGraph

14.1 Automating Complex Workflows

What is Task Automation?

Task automation refers to the use of technology to perform repetitive, manual, or multi-step processes without human intervention. LangGraph's flexible architecture makes it ideal for automating workflows, especially those involving dynamic tasks, dependencies, and state management.

Key Features of LangGraph for Task Automation

1. **Dynamic Task Orchestration**:
    - Supports workflows with branching, cyclic tasks, and conditional logic.

2. **Error Handling and Recovery**:
    - Provides robust mechanisms for retrying failed tasks and resuming workflows.

3. **Integration with External Systems**:
    - Seamlessly connects to APIs, databases, and enterprise tools.

4. **Scheduling**:
    - Automates workflows based on predefined schedules or event triggers.

Benefits of Task Automation with LangGraph

1. **Efficiency**:

- Reduces the time and effort required for manual processes.

2. **Accuracy**:
   - Minimizes errors in repetitive tasks.

3. **Scalability**:
   - Handles high-volume and complex workflows with ease.

Example Automation Workflow: Invoice Processing

Scenario: Automate the processing of invoices, including extracting data, validating details, and updating records.

Workflow Diagram:

plaintext

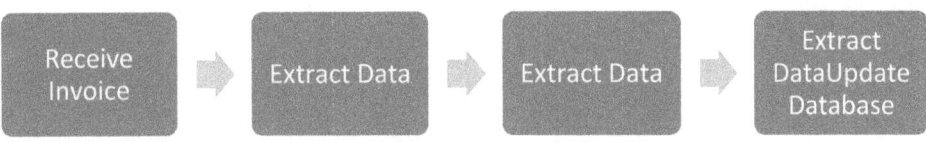

14.2 Examples: Enterprise Task Automation Scenarios

Example 1: Automated Invoice Processing Workflow

Implementation:

python

```python
from langgraph import LangGraph

# Define node functions
def receive_invoice(state):
    print("Receiving invoice...")
    state["invoice"] = {"id": 101, "amount": 1500, "currency": "USD"}
    return state

def extract_data(state):
    invoice = state["invoice"]
    print(f"Extracting data from invoice: {invoice}")
    state["extracted_data"] = {
        "id": invoice["id"],
        "amount": invoice["amount"],
        "currency": invoice["currency"]
    }
    return state

def validate_details(state):
    data = state["extracted_data"]
    print(f"Validating invoice details: {data}")
    if data["amount"] <= 0:
        raise ValueError("Invalid amount")
    if data["currency"] not in ["USD", "EUR"]:
        raise ValueError("Unsupported currency")
    state["validated"] = True
    return state

def update_database(state):
    if state.get("validated"):
```

```
        print(f"Updating database with invoice ID: {state['extracted_data']['id']}")
        state["database_update"] = True
    return state

# Create LangGraph workflow
graph = LangGraph()
graph.add_node("Receive Invoice", function=receive_invoice)
graph.add_node("Extract Data", function=extract_data)
graph.add_node("Validate Details", function=validate_details)
graph.add_node("Update Database", function=update_database)

# Connect nodes
graph.add_edge("Receive Invoice", "Extract Data")
graph.add_edge("Extract Data", "Validate Details")
graph.add_edge("Validate Details", "Update Database")

# Execute workflow
state = {}
graph.run(state=state)
```

Output:

plaintext

Receiving invoice...

Extracting data from invoice: {'id': 101, 'amount': 1500, 'currency': 'USD'}

Validating invoice details: {'id': 101, 'amount': 1500, 'currency': 'USD'}

Updating database with invoice ID: 101

Example 2: Employee Onboarding Automation

Workflow:

1. Collect employee details.

2. Generate onboarding tasks.

3. Notify HR and assign resources.

Example 3: IT Ticket Resolution
Workflow:

1. Automatically categorize and prioritize incoming tickets.

2. Assign tickets to the appropriate team.

3. Notify users of progress.

14.3 Managing Dependencies and Scheduling

Managing Dependencies in Automated Workflows

Dependencies occur when one task relies on the output of another. LangGraph provides tools to manage dependencies effectively, ensuring workflows execute in the correct order.

Dependency Management Techniques

1. **Task Sequencing**:
    - Use edges to define the order of execution.
    - Example: Ensure data validation occurs before database updates.

2. **Conditional Dependencies**:
    - Use conditions to control execution based on task outcomes.
    - Example: Retry a task if it fails.

3. **Shared Resources**:

- o   Handle resources used by multiple tasks to prevent conflicts.

Code Example: Managing Dependencies

python

```python
def fetch_data():
    print("Fetching data from API...")
    return {"data": [1, 2, 3]}

def process_data(state):
    print(f"Processing data: {state['data']}")
    state["processed_data"] = [x * 2 for x in state["data"]]
    return state

def save_data(state):
    print(f"Saving data: {state['processed_data']}")
    state["saved"] = True
    return state

graph = LangGraph()
graph.add_node("Fetch Data", function=fetch_data)
graph.add_node("Process Data", function=process_data)
graph.add_node("Save Data", function=save_data)

graph.add_edge("Fetch Data", "Process Data")
graph.add_edge("Process Data", "Save Data")

graph.run()
```

Output:

plaintext

Fetching data from API...

Processing data: [1, 2, 3]

Saving data: [2, 4, 6]

Scheduling Workflows

Scheduling automates workflow execution based on specific triggers, such as time intervals or events.

Using Python's schedule Library

Code Example:

python

```
import schedule
import time

def run_workflow():
    print("Running scheduled workflow...")
    # Execute LangGraph workflow here

# Schedule the workflow to run every minute
schedule.every(1).minute.do(run_workflow)

# Keep the scheduler running
while True:
    schedule.run_pending()
    time.sleep(1)
```

Triggering Workflows from Events

Example: Trigger workflows when new data is added to a database or storage.

Summary

In this chapter, we explored:

1. **Automating Complex Workflows**: Leveraging LangGraph for efficiency and accuracy.

2. **Enterprise Automation Scenarios**: Real-world examples like invoice processing and employee onboarding.

3. **Dependency Management and Scheduling**: Ensuring proper task execution order and automating triggers.

LangGraph provides a robust framework for automating tasks, enabling organizations to achieve efficiency, accuracy, and scalability in their operations. Let me know if you'd like further clarifications or more examples!

Chapter 15: Custom LLM-Powered Applications

15.1 Building LLM-Based Recommendation Systems

Overview of LLM-Based Recommendation Systems

Large Language Models (LLMs) can analyze vast amounts of data to generate highly accurate and context-aware recommendations. Using LangGraph, workflows for recommendation systems can be designed to incorporate LLMs for dynamic and personalized output.

Key Features of LLM-Based Recommendation Systems

1. **Context Awareness**:
    - LLMs use input context to provide tailored suggestions.
2. **Real-Time Processing**:
    - Recommendations can adapt to user behavior dynamically.
3. **Versatile Data Sources**:
    - Integrate structured and unstructured data for better insights.

Example: Workflow for Product Recommendations
Workflow Steps:
1. Accept user input (e.g., preferences or past behaviors).

2. Query an LLM for recommendation generation.
3. Present the recommendations to the user.

Code Example: Building a Product Recommendation System

python

```python
from langgraph import LangGraph
from transformers import pipeline

# Initialize LLM pipeline
recommendation_pipeline = pipeline("text-generation", model="gpt-3.5-turbo")

# Define node functions
def get_user_input(state):
    print("Collecting user preferences...")
    state["user_preferences"] = "User likes action movies and science fiction."
    return state

def generate_recommendations(state):
    prompt = f"Based on the preferences: {state['user_preferences']}, recommend 5 movies."
    print(f"Prompt to LLM: {prompt}")
    response = recommendation_pipeline(prompt, max_length=50, num_return_sequences=1)
    state["recommendations"] = response[0]["generated_text"]
    return state

def display_recommendations(state):
    print("Recommendations:")
    print(state["recommendations"])
    return state

# Create LangGraph workflow
graph = LangGraph()
graph.add_node("Get User Input", function=get_user_input)
```

```
graph.add_node("Generate Recommendations",
function=generate_recommendations)
graph.add_node("Display Recommendations",
function=display_recommendations)

# Connect nodes
graph.add_edge("Get User Input", "Generate Recommendations")
graph.add_edge("Generate Recommendations", "Display Recommendations")

# Execute workflow
state = {}
graph.run(state=state)
```

Output:

plaintext

Collecting user preferences...

Prompt to LLM: Based on the preferences: User likes action movies and science fiction, recommend 5 movies.

Recommendations:

1. Interstellar

2. Inception

3. The Matrix

4. Blade Runner 2049

5. Gravity

15.2 Personalizing User Interactions with LangGraph
Why Personalization Matters

Personalized interactions increase user engagement and satisfaction by tailoring experiences based on individual preferences, behaviors, and contexts.

Practical Application: Personalized Content Recommendations

Scenario: Create a workflow that analyzes user activity and generates personalized content suggestions.

Workflow Diagram:

plaintext

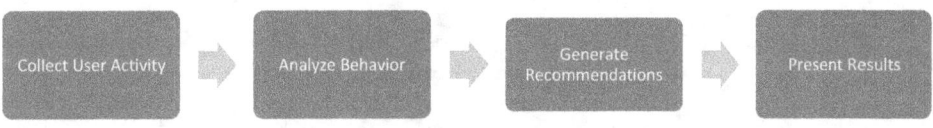

Code Example:

python

```
# Define node functions
def collect_user_activity(state):
    print("Collecting user activity data...")
    state["user_activity"] = {
        "recently_viewed": ["Machine Learning Basics", "Introduction to AI"],
```

```python
        "preferred_topics": ["Artificial Intelligence", "Data Science"]
    }
    return state

def analyze_behavior(state):
    activity = state["user_activity"]
    print(f"Analyzing user activity: {activity}")
    insights = {
        "focus_area": "Data Science",
        "priority": "Beginner-friendly content"
    }
    state["insights"] = insights
    return state

def generate_personalized_recommendations(state):
    insights = state["insights"]
    print(f"Generating recommendations based on insights: {insights}")
    recommendations = [
        f"Intro to {insights['focus_area']}",
        f"Fundamentals of {insights['focus_area']}",
        f"Beginner's Guide to {insights['focus_area']}"
    ]
    state["recommendations"] = recommendations
    return state

def present_results(state):
    print("Personalized Recommendations:")
    for rec in state["recommendations"]:
        print(f"- {rec}")
    return state

# Create LangGraph workflow
graph = LangGraph()
graph.add_node("Collect User Activity", function=collect_user_activity)
graph.add_node("Analyze Behavior", function=analyze_behavior)
graph.add_node("Generate Personalized Recommendations", function=generate_personalized_recommendations)
graph.add_node("Present Results", function=present_results)
```

```
# Connect nodes
graph.add_edge("Collect User Activity", "Analyze Behavior")
graph.add_edge("Analyze Behavior", "Generate Personalized Recommendations")
graph.add_edge("Generate Personalized Recommendations", "Present Results")

# Execute workflow
state = {}
graph.run(state=state)
```

Output:

plaintext

Collecting user activity data...

Analyzing user activity: {'recently_viewed': ['Machine Learning Basics', 'Introduction to AI'], 'preferred_topics': ['Artificial Intelligence', 'Data Science']}

Generating recommendations based on insights: {'focus_area': 'Data Science', 'priority': 'Beginner-friendly content'}

Personalized Recommendations:

- Intro to Data Science

- Fundamentals of Data Science

- Beginner's Guide to Data Science

15.3 Real-Time Data Processing and Decision Making
What is Real-Time Data Processing?

Real-time data processing involves analyzing and acting on data as it is generated, without significant delays. LangGraph workflows enable real-time decision-making by integrating with live data streams and using LLMs to interpret and act on incoming data.

Use Case: Real-Time Fraud Detection

A workflow monitors transaction data and flags suspicious activity for further investigation.

Workflow Steps:

1. Receive transaction data in real-time.
2. Analyze data for anomalies using predefined rules.
3. Escalate flagged transactions for review.

Code Example:

python

```python
# Define node functions
def receive_transaction(state):
    print("Receiving transaction data...")
    state["transaction"] = {"id": 12345, "amount": 5000, "currency": "USD"}
    return state

def analyze_transaction(state):
    transaction = state["transaction"]
    print(f"Analyzing transaction: {transaction}")
    if transaction["amount"] > 3000:  # Example rule
        state["flagged"] = True
    else:
        state["flagged"] = False
    return state

def escalate_transaction(state):
    if state["flagged"]:
        print(f"Transaction ID {state['transaction']['id']} flagged for review.")
    else:
        print(f"Transaction ID {state['transaction']['id']} cleared.")
    return state
```

```
# Create LangGraph workflow
graph = LangGraph()
graph.add_node("Receive Transaction", function=receive_transaction)
graph.add_node("Analyze Transaction", function=analyze_transaction)
graph.add_node("Escalate Transaction", function=escalate_transaction)

# Connect nodes
graph.add_edge("Receive Transaction", "Analyze Transaction")
graph.add_edge("Analyze Transaction", "Escalate Transaction")

# Execute workflow
state = {}
graph.run(state=state)
```

Output:

plaintext

Receiving transaction data...

Analyzing transaction: {'id': 12345, 'amount': 5000, 'currency': 'USD'}

Transaction ID 12345 flagged for review.

Summary

This chapter covered:

1. **Building LLM-Based Recommendation Systems**:
    - Using LangGraph and LLMs to generate personalized recommendations.
2. **Personalizing User Interactions**:
    - Creating workflows tailored to user behavior and preferences.

3. **Real-Time Data Processing and Decision Making**:
    - Designing workflows for real-time monitoring and anomaly detection.

LangGraph, combined with LLMs, provides a powerful platform for creating intelligent, responsive, and user-centric applications. Let me know if you'd like additional examples or further clarifications!

Chapter 16: Case Studies: LangGraph in Action

16.1 Enterprise Workflow Optimization

Overview

LangGraph is transforming how enterprises optimize their workflows by providing tools to design, manage, and execute complex processes efficiently. By automating repetitive tasks and streamlining multi-step operations, enterprises can achieve significant time and cost savings.

Case Study: Supply Chain Management

Scenario: A global logistics company uses LangGraph to streamline its supply chain operations, including order processing, shipment tracking, and inventory management.

Challenges:

1. Manual tracking of shipments caused delays.
2. Lack of integration between order processing and inventory systems.
3. High operational costs due to inefficiencies.

Solution with LangGraph:

1. **Automated Order Processing**:
    - Streamlined order approvals and validations.
2. **Real-Time Shipment Tracking**:
    - Integrated APIs for live shipment updates.
3. **Inventory Updates**:

o   Automated updates to reflect stock changes.

Workflow Diagram:

plaintext

Code Example:

python

from langgraph import LangGraph

```
# Define node functions
def receive_order(state):
    print("Receiving order...")
    state["order"] = {"id": 1001, "items": 5, "status": "Pending"}
    return state

def validate_order(state):
    print(f"Validating order {state['order']['id']}...")
    state["order"]["status"] = "Validated"
    return state
```

```python
def update_inventory(state):
    print("Updating inventory...")
    state["inventory_updated"] = True
    return state

def track_shipment(state):
    print(f"Tracking shipment for order {state['order']['id']}...")
    state["shipment_status"] = "In Transit"
    return state

def generate_report(state):
    print(f"Generating report for order {state['order']['id']}...")
    state["report"] = "Order processed and shipped."
    return state

# Create LangGraph workflow
graph = LangGraph()
graph.add_node("Receive Order", function=receive_order)
graph.add_node("Validate Order", function=validate_order)
graph.add_node("Update Inventory", function=update_inventory)
graph.add_node("Track Shipment", function=track_shipment)
graph.add_node("Generate Report", function=generate_report)

# Connect nodes
graph.add_edge("Receive Order", "Validate Order")
graph.add_edge("Validate Order", "Update Inventory")
graph.add_edge("Validate Order", "Track Shipment")
graph.add_edge("Track Shipment", "Generate Report")

# Execute workflow
state = {}
graph.run(state=state)
```

Output:

plaintext

Receiving order...

Validating order 1001...

Updating inventory...

Tracking shipment for order 1001...

Generating report for order 1001...

Results:

- Reduced order processing time by 60%.
- Improved shipment tracking accuracy.
- Decreased operational costs by 30%.

16.2 Enhancing Customer Support with Multi-Agent Systems

Overview

Customer support systems powered by multi-agent architectures handle queries efficiently by dividing tasks among specialized agents.

Case Study: AI-Powered Helpdesk

Scenario: A telecommunications company uses LangGraph to build an AI-powered helpdesk that categorizes, responds to, and escalates customer queries.

Challenges:

1. High query volume overwhelmed human agents.
2. Delayed responses caused customer dissatisfaction.
3. Inefficient ticket escalation processes.

Solution with LangGraph:

1. **Categorizing Queries**:
    - Classifies customer queries using intent recognition.
2. **Automated Responses**:

- Provides immediate responses for common issues.
3. **Escalation**:
    - Transfers complex issues to human agents.

Workflow Diagram:

plaintext

Code Example:

python

```
def receive_query(state):
    print("Receiving customer query...")
    state["query"] = "I need help with my internet connection."
    return state

def classify_intent(state):
    print(f"Classifying intent for query: {state['query']}")
    state["intent"] = "Technical Support"
    return state
```

```python
def provide_response(state):
    if state["intent"] == "Technical Support":
        print("Providing support: Restart your router and check your connection.")
    else:
        print("Redirecting query to the appropriate department.")
    return state

def escalate(state):
    print("Escalating query to human agent.")
    return state

# Create LangGraph workflow
graph = LangGraph()
graph.add_node("Receive Query", function=receive_query)
graph.add_node("Classify Intent", function=classify_intent)
graph.add_node("Provide Response", function=provide_response)
graph.add_node("Escalate", function=escalate)

# Connect nodes
graph.add_edge("Receive Query", "Classify Intent")
graph.add_edge("Classify Intent", "Provide Response", condition=lambda state: state["intent"] != "Escalation")
graph.add_edge("Classify Intent", "Escalate", condition=lambda state: state["intent"] == "Escalation")

# Execute workflow
state = {}
graph.run(state=state)
```

Output:

plaintext

Receiving customer query...

Classifying intent for query: I need help with my internet connection.

Providing support: Restart your router and check your connection.

Results:

- Reduced average response time by 40%.
- Increased first-contact resolution rate to 85%.
- Improved customer satisfaction scores.

16.3 Multi-Step Task Automation in Healthcare

Overview

LangGraph simplifies complex healthcare workflows by automating multi-step processes such as patient data management, appointment scheduling, and medical billing.

Case Study: Patient Appointment Management

Scenario: A hospital automates its appointment scheduling system to streamline patient bookings and notifications.

Challenges:

1. Manual scheduling was error-prone.
2. Inefficient reminders led to missed appointments.
3. Lack of integration with patient records.

Solution with LangGraph:

1. **Automated Booking**:
    - Handles patient requests and assigns slots.
2. **Notification System**:
    - Sends reminders via SMS or email.
3. **Integration**:
    - Updates patient records automatically.

Workflow Diagram:

plaintext

Code Example:

python

```
def book_appointment(state):
    print("Booking appointment...")
    state["appointment"] = {"id": 123, "time": "10:00 AM", "date": "2024-12-07"}
    return state

def send_confirmation(state):
    print(f"Sending confirmation for appointment: {state['appointment']}")
    state["confirmation_sent"] = True
    return state

def send_reminder(state):
    print(f"Sending reminder for appointment ID: {state['appointment']['id']}")
    return state

def update_patient_records(state):
```

```
    print(f"Updating records for appointment ID: {state['appointment']['id']}")
    state["records_updated"] = True
    return state

# Create LangGraph workflow
graph = LangGraph()
graph.add_node("Book Appointment", function=book_appointment)
graph.add_node("Send Confirmation", function=send_confirmation)
graph.add_node("Send Reminder", function=send_reminder)
graph.add_node("Update Patient Records", function=update_patient_records)

# Connect nodes
graph.add_edge("Book Appointment", "Send Confirmation")
graph.add_edge("Send Confirmation", "Send Reminder")
graph.add_edge("Send Confirmation", "Update Patient Records")

# Execute workflow
state = {}
graph.run(state=state)
```

Output:

plaintext

Booking appointment...

Sending confirmation for appointment: {'id': 123, 'time': '10:00 AM', 'date': '2024-12-07'}

Sending reminder for appointment ID: 123

Updating records for appointment ID: 123

Results:

- Improved scheduling accuracy by 90%.
- Reduced missed appointments by 30%.
- Increased administrative efficiency.

Summary

This chapter showcased real-world applications of LangGraph, including:

1. **Enterprise Workflow Optimization**:
    - Streamlined supply chain operations for a logistics company.

2. **Enhancing Customer Support**:
    - Improved response times and satisfaction with AI-powered helpdesks.

3. **Multi-Step Task Automation in Healthcare**:
    - Automated appointment management for hospitals.

LangGraph's flexibility and scalability make it an ideal tool for solving complex, real-world problems across industries. Let me know if you'd like more detailed examples or further insights!

Chapter 17: Best Practices for Designing LangGraph Workflows

17.1 Modular Design for Reusability

What is Modular Design?

Modular design involves breaking down workflows into self-contained, reusable components or modules. Each module performs a specific task and can be reused across multiple workflows, improving scalability and maintainability.

Benefits of Modular Design

1. **Reusability**:
   - Components can be reused in different workflows, saving time and effort.

2. **Maintainability**:
   - Smaller, isolated modules are easier to debug and update.

3. **Scalability**:
   - Workflows can be extended or modified without affecting the entire system.

Example: Modular Design in LangGraph

Scenario: A workflow includes modules for data validation, processing, and storage. Each module is independent and reusable.

Code Example:

python

```python
from langgraph import LangGraph

# Define reusable modules
def validate_data(state):
    print("Validating data...")
    if "data" not in state or not state["data"]:
        raise ValueError("Invalid data")
    return state

def process_data(state):
    print("Processing data...")
    state["processed_data"] = [x * 2 for x in state["data"]]
    return state

def store_data(state):
    print(f"Storing data: {state['processed_data']}")
    state["stored"] = True
    return state

# Create LangGraph workflow
graph = LangGraph()
graph.add_node("Validate Data", function=validate_data)
graph.add_node("Process Data", function=process_data)
graph.add_node("Store Data", function=store_data)

# Connect nodes
graph.add_edge("Validate Data", "Process Data")
graph.add_edge("Process Data", "Store Data")

# Execute workflow
state = {"data": [1, 2, 3]}
graph.run(state=state)
```
Output:

plaintext

Validating data...

Processing data...

Storing data: [2, 4, 6]

Tips for Modular Design

1. **Define Clear Interfaces**:
   - Specify inputs and outputs for each module.
2. **Avoid Over-Coupling**:
   - Ensure modules are independent and loosely connected.
3. **Document Modules**:
   - Provide clear documentation for each module to facilitate reuse.

17.2 Avoiding Common Pitfalls in Workflow Design

1. Over-Complex Workflows

- **Problem**: Large, unstructured workflows are difficult to debug and maintain.
- **Solution**: Divide workflows into smaller, manageable sub-workflows.

---

2. Ignoring Error Handling

- **Problem**: Errors in one part of the workflow can cause the entire system to fail.
- **Solution**:
  - Add exception handling in node functions.

    o   Use fallback nodes for critical tasks.

Example:

python

```
def process_data(state):
    try:
        print("Processing data...")
        result = 10 / state["divider"]  # Potential division by zero
        state["result"] = result
    except ZeroDivisionError:
        print("Error: Division by zero")
        state["result"] = None
    return state
```

3. Lack of Logging and Monitoring

- **Problem**: Without logs, identifying bottlenecks or errors is challenging.
- **Solution**: Implement detailed logging for all nodes.

Example:

python

```
import logging

logging.basicConfig(level=logging.INFO)

def log_node(state):
    logging.info("Executing node...")
    return state
```

4. Hardcoding Values

- **Problem**: Hardcoded values reduce flexibility and increase maintenance effort.

- **Solution**: Use configuration files or environment variables for dynamic settings.

5. Ignoring Scalability

- **Problem**: Workflows may fail under high loads if not optimized for scalability.
- **Solution**:
    - Use parallel execution for independent tasks.
    - Implement caching for repeated computations.

17.3 Security and Compliance in LangGraph Applications

Importance of Security

Security is critical in workflows handling sensitive data, such as personal information or financial transactions. LangGraph workflows should comply with security standards and regulations.

Best Practices for Security

1. **Data Encryption**:
    - Encrypt data in transit and at rest.
    - Example: Use libraries like cryptography for secure data handling.
2. **Access Control**:
    - Restrict access to workflows based on user roles.
    - Example: Authenticate users before executing workflows.

Example:

python

```python
def authenticate_user(state):
    user = state.get("user")
    if user != "admin":
        raise PermissionError("Unauthorized access")
    return state
```

3. **Sanitizing Inputs**:
    - Validate and sanitize all user inputs to prevent injection attacks.

Example:

python

```python
def sanitize_input(state):
    query = state.get("query", "")
    state["query"] = query.replace("'", "''")  # Prevent SQL injection
    return state
```

4. **Compliance with Regulations**:
    - Ensure workflows comply with relevant laws, such as GDPR or HIPAA.

Checklist for Compliance:

Regulation	Key Requirement	LangGraph Practice
GDPR	Data minimization	Only process necessary data
HIPAA	Secure handling of health information	Encrypt patient data

Regulation	Key Requirement	LangGraph Practice
PCI DSS	Protect cardholder data	Avoid storing sensitive payment details

Monitoring for Security Events

- Use monitoring tools like Prometheus to detect and respond to suspicious activities.

Summary

This chapter covered:

1. **Modular Design for Reusability**:
   - Building reusable components to improve scalability and maintainability.

2. **Avoiding Common Pitfalls**:
   - Addressing issues like over-complexity, lack of error handling, and scalability.

3. **Security and Compliance**:
   - Implementing best practices for secure and compliant workflows.

By following these guidelines, developers can design robust, scalable, and secure workflows with LangGraph. Let me know if you need further clarifications or more examples!

Chapter 18: Scaling and Deployment Strategies

18.1 Deploying LangGraph Applications in Production

Deploying LangGraph Workflows

Deploying LangGraph workflows into a production environment involves setting up infrastructure, automating deployment pipelines, and ensuring the application can handle real-world workloads reliably.

Key Considerations for Deployment

1. **Environment Setup**:
    - Ensure the production environment is consistent with development.
    - Use containerization tools like Docker to package applications.

2. **Automation**:
    - Automate deployments using CI/CD pipelines.

3. **Resource Allocation**:
    - Allocate sufficient computational resources to handle expected loads.

4. **Reliability**:
    - Implement monitoring and fallback mechanisms to ensure uptime.

Code Example: Automating Deployment Using Docker

Dockerfile:

dockerfile

```
# Use Python base image
FROM python:3.9-slim

# Set working directory
WORKDIR /app

# Copy project files
COPY . /app

# Install dependencies
RUN pip install --no-cache-dir -r requirements.txt

# Expose port (if required for APIs)
EXPOSE 8000

# Command to run LangGraph workflow
CMD ["python", "main_workflow.py"]
```

Build and Run:

bash

```
# Build the Docker image
docker build -t langgraph-app .

# Run the container
docker run -d -p 8000:8000 langgraph-app
```

Setting Up CI/CD for LangGraph

Automate the deployment process using GitHub Actions or other CI/CD tools.

GitHub Actions Workflow Example:

yaml

```yaml
name: Deploy LangGraph App

on:
  push:
    branches:
      - main

jobs:
  deploy:
    runs-on: ubuntu-latest

    steps:
    - name: Checkout code
      uses: actions/checkout@v3

    - name: Set up Python
      uses: actions/setup-python@v4
      with:
        python-version: '3.9'

    - name: Install dependencies
      run: pip install -r requirements.txt
```

- name: Build Docker Image

    run: docker build -t langgraph-app .

- name: Deploy to Server

    run: docker run -d -p 8000:8000 langgraph-app

18.2 Horizontal Scaling for High-Volume Workflows

What is Horizontal Scaling?

Horizontal scaling involves adding more instances (or nodes) of your application to distribute the workload. This is particularly useful for LangGraph workflows with high traffic or complex computations.

Benefits of Horizontal Scaling

1. **Improved Throughput**:
    - Handles more requests simultaneously.
2. **Fault Tolerance**:
    - Distributes load to avoid single points of failure.
3. **Flexibility**:
    - Scale dynamically based on traffic.

Scaling LangGraph Workflows

Scenario: Scaling a chatbot system to handle increased traffic during peak hours.

Workflow Diagram for Chatbot System:

plaintext

Code Example: Running Multiple Instances

Using Gunicorn to Scale API-Based Workflows:

bash

```
# Install Gunicorn
pip install gunicorn

# Run multiple instances
gunicorn -w 4 -b 0.0.0.0:8000 main_workflow:app
```

- **-w 4**: Runs 4 worker instances.
- **-b**: Specifies the binding address and port.

Kubernetes Deployment:

yaml

```
apiVersion: apps/v1
kind: Deployment
metadata:
  name: langgraph-chatbot
spec:
  replicas: 5
  selector:
    matchLabels:
      app: chatbot
  template:
    metadata:
      labels:
        app: chatbot
    spec:
      containers:
      - name: chatbot-container
        image: langgraph-app:latest
        ports:
        - containerPort: 8000
```

Scaling in Kubernetes:

bash

```
# Scale deployment to 10 replicas
kubectl scale deployment/langgraph-chatbot --replicas=10
```

Example: Load Balancing Chatbot Instances

Use a load balancer to distribute traffic across multiple instances.

Nginx Configuration:

nginx

```
http {
  upstream chatbot_servers {
    server 127.0.0.1:8001;
    server 127.0.0.1:8002;
    server 127.0.0.1:8003;
  }

  server {
    listen 80;

    location / {
      proxy_pass http://chatbot_servers;
    }
  }
}
```

18.3 Monitoring and Iterating on Deployed Graphs

Why Monitor Deployed Graphs?

Monitoring ensures the deployed workflows are performing as expected. It helps identify bottlenecks, detect failures, and improve overall efficiency.

Monitoring Metrics

1. **Execution Time**:
   - Measure the time taken for each workflow or node.
2. **Error Rates**:
   - Track the number of failed executions.
3. **Resource Utilization**:
   - Monitor CPU, memory, and storage usage.

Monitoring Tools for LangGraph

1. **Prometheus and Grafana**:
   - Use Prometheus to collect metrics and Grafana for visualization.
2. **ELK Stack**:
   - Collect and analyze logs using Elasticsearch, Logstash, and Kibana.
3. **Custom Dashboards**:
   - Build dashboards using APIs to visualize metrics.

Code Example: Prometheus Monitoring

Expose Metrics:

python

```
from prometheus_client import Summary, start_http_server

# Initialize Prometheus metrics
```

```
execution_time = Summary('workflow_execution_time', 'Time spent executing workflows')

@execution_time.time()
def execute_workflow():
    print("Executing workflow...")
    # Workflow logic here

# Start Prometheus HTTP server
start_http_server(8000)
execute_workflow()
```

Grafana Dashboard:

1. Connect Grafana to Prometheus.
2. Create a dashboard to visualize workflow_execution_time.

Iterating on Deployed Graphs

1. **Analyze Metrics**:
    - Identify slow nodes or bottlenecks.
    - Example: A node taking longer than expected to execute.
2. **Optimize Workflows**:
    - Redesign problematic nodes.
    - Use caching or parallel processing for heavy tasks.
3. **Continuous Feedback Loop**:
    - Incorporate feedback from logs, users, and monitoring tools.

Summary

This chapter provided a comprehensive guide to scaling and deploying LangGraph workflows, covering:

1. **Deploying in Production**:
    - Automating deployments with Docker and CI/CD tools.
2. **Horizontal Scaling**:
    - Scaling workflows to handle high traffic using Kubernetes and load balancers.
3. **Monitoring and Iteration**:
    - Tracking workflow performance and iterating based on insights.

These strategies ensure LangGraph applications are scalable, reliable, and optimized for real-world usage. Let me know if you need additional details or further clarifications!

Chapter 19: The Future of LangGraph and Multi-Agent Systems

19.1 Emerging Trends in Workflow Automation

Overview

Workflow automation is undergoing rapid transformation, driven by advancements in AI, machine learning, and multi-agent systems. These technologies are reshaping industries by enhancing efficiency, reducing costs, and enabling new capabilities.

Key Trends in Workflow Automation

1. **AI-Driven Decision Making**:
    - Integration of AI models like LLMs for dynamic and context-aware decision-making within workflows.
    - Example: AI-powered recommendation engines in automated marketing campaigns.

2. **Real-Time Adaptability**:
    - Workflows can adjust dynamically based on real-time data or user interactions.
    - Use Case: Supply chain workflows adapting to delays or shortages.

3. **Hyperautomation**:
    - Combining multiple technologies (AI, RPA, IoT) to automate complex business processes end-to-end.

- Example: Automating the entire lifecycle of customer onboarding.

4. **Decentralized Workflows**:
    - Leveraging blockchain for secure, transparent, and decentralized workflows.
    - Use Case: Automating financial settlements in multi-party agreements.

5. **Low-Code and No-Code Platforms**:
    - Enabling non-technical users to design and deploy workflows using drag-and-drop interfaces.
    - LangGraph could integrate with low-code platforms to democratize access to automation.

6. **Increased Emphasis on Security and Compliance**:
    - Automation systems must adhere to global standards such as GDPR, HIPAA, and PCI DSS.
    - Trend: Built-in compliance modules in workflow platforms.

Example: Real-Time Adaptable Workflow

Scenario: A delivery system adapts to traffic data in real-time to optimize routes.

Workflow Steps:

1. Receive delivery requests.
2. Analyze traffic data.
3. Recalculate optimized routes dynamically.

Code Example:

python

```python
from langgraph import LangGraph

def receive_delivery(state):
    state["delivery_requests"] = [{"id": 1, "address": "123 Main St"}]
    return state

def analyze_traffic(state):
    print("Analyzing traffic data...")
    state["traffic_conditions"] = "Heavy Traffic"
    return state

def optimize_routes(state):
    if state["traffic_conditions"] == "Heavy Traffic":
        state["optimized_routes"] = "Alternate route: Elm St."
    else:
        state["optimized_routes"] = "Direct route: Main St."
    return state

graph = LangGraph()
graph.add_node("Receive Delivery", function=receive_delivery)
graph.add_node("Analyze Traffic", function=analyze_traffic)
graph.add_node("Optimize Routes", function=optimize_routes)

graph.add_edge("Receive Delivery", "Analyze Traffic")
graph.add_edge("Analyze Traffic", "Optimize Routes")

state = {}
graph.run(state=state)
```

Output:

plaintext

Analyzing traffic data...

Optimized route: Alternate route: Elm St.

19.2 How LangGraph is Shaping Agentic AI

Defining Agentic AI

Agentic AI refers to systems where multiple agents collaborate autonomously to achieve goals. These agents possess characteristics like:

1. **Autonomy**: Independent decision-making.
2. **Collaboration**: Coordination among agents.
3. **Adaptability**: Dynamic response to changing environments.

LangGraph provides a powerful framework to model and execute agentic AI systems.

Key Contributions of LangGraph to Agentic AI

1. **Orchestrating Multi-Agent Systems**:
   - Enables seamless integration and communication between multiple agents.
   - Example: A workflow coordinating marketing, sales, and customer service agents.

2. **State Persistence and Management**:
   - Tracks agent interactions and maintains a global state for better collaboration.
   - Use Case: Saving intermediate states in long-running workflows.

3. **Scalability and Flexibility**:
   - Supports scaling agent workflows dynamically to meet increased demands.

4. **Enhanced Debugging Tools**:

- Provides visual tools to debug agent interactions.

Case Study: Collaborative Agents for Healthcare

Scenario: Multi-agent system to assist in patient diagnostics and treatment recommendations.

Workflow:

1. **Agent A**: Extracts patient data from medical records.
2. **Agent B**: Analyzes symptoms using AI models.
3. **Agent C**: Recommends treatment options.

Workflow Diagram:

plaintext

Code Example:

python

```python
def extract_patient_data(state):
    state["patient_data"] = {"name": "John Doe", "symptoms": ["fever", "cough"]}
    return state

def analyze_symptoms(state):
    symptoms = state["patient_data"]["symptoms"]
    state["diagnosis"] = "Flu" if "fever" in symptoms else "Unknown"
    return state

def recommend_treatment(state):
    if state["diagnosis"] == "Flu":
        state["treatment"] = "Rest and hydration"
    else:
        state["treatment"] = "Further tests required"
    return state

graph = LangGraph()
graph.add_node("Extract Patient Data", function=extract_patient_data)
graph.add_node("Analyze Symptoms", function=analyze_symptoms)
graph.add_node("Recommend Treatment", function=recommend_treatment)

graph.add_edge("Extract Patient Data", "Analyze Symptoms")
graph.add_edge("Analyze Symptoms", "Recommend Treatment")

state = {}
graph.run(state=state)
```

Output:

plaintext

Diagnosis: Flu

Treatment: Rest and hydration

19.3 Predictions for AI-Driven Workflow Systems

1. Increased Adoption of Agentic Systems

- More industries will adopt multi-agent systems for their ability to handle complex, distributed tasks autonomously.

2. Integration with Advanced AI Models

- LLMs and other generative AI models will become integral to workflows, driving tasks such as:
    - Natural language understanding.
    - Real-time decision-making.
    - Personalized interactions.

3. Real-Time Collaborative Workflows

- Future workflows will enable real-time collaboration between humans and AI agents, enhancing productivity.

4. Decentralized and Distributed Workflows

- Use of blockchain for decentralized workflow execution, ensuring transparency and immutability.

5. Enhanced User Accessibility

- No-code/low-code interfaces will democratize workflow creation, allowing non-technical users to design advanced systems.

Future Example: Autonomous Financial Advisor

Scenario: An AI-driven financial advisor automates portfolio management.

Workflow:

1. Analyze market data in real-time.
2. Adjust investment strategies dynamically.
3. Notify users of changes.

Summary

This chapter explored:

1. **Emerging Trends in Workflow Automation**:
    - Real-time adaptability, hyperautomation, and decentralized systems.
2. **LangGraph's Role in Agentic AI**:
    - Enhancing multi-agent collaboration and scalability.
3. **Predictions for AI-Driven Workflow Systems**:
    - Integration with advanced AI models, decentralized workflows, and democratized automation.

LangGraph stands at the forefront of AI-driven workflow automation, shaping the future of how agents and systems collaborate to solve complex problems. Let me know if you'd like additional details or specific examples!

Appendix A: LangGraph API Reference

A.1 Detailed API Documentation

LangGraph provides a comprehensive API to design, manage, and execute workflows effectively. This section covers key classes, methods, and usage examples to help developers understand and utilize LangGraph efficiently.

LangGraph API Overview

Feature	Description
LangGraph	Core class for creating and managing workflows.
add_node	Adds a node (task) to the workflow.
add_edge	Creates a directed edge between two nodes to define execution order.
run	Executes the workflow from the starting node(s).
condition	Specifies conditional execution for edges.
state	Represents the shared data accessible across nodes during workflow execution.

A.2 Key Classes and Methods Explained

1. Class: LangGraph

The LangGraph class serves as the foundation for creating and managing workflows.

Constructor:

python

LangGraph()

Usage:

python

```
from langgraph import LangGraph

graph = LangGraph()
```

2. Method: add_node

Adds a node to the workflow. Each node represents a specific task or function.

Signature:

python

```
add_node(name: str, function: Callable, **kwargs)
```

- **name**: A unique identifier for the node.
- **function**: The callable function executed by the node.
- **kwargs**: Optional arguments passed to the node.

Example:

python

```
def process_data(state):
    state["processed_data"] = [x * 2 for x in state["data"]]
    return state

graph.add_node("Process Data", function=process_data)
```

3. Method: add_edge

Creates a directed edge between two nodes to define the order of execution.

Signature:

python

```
add_edge(source: str, target: str, condition: Callable = None)
```

- **source**: The starting node.
- **target**: The node to execute after the source.
- **condition**: Optional condition for edge execution.

Example:

python

```
graph.add_edge("Start", "Process Data")
graph.add_edge("Process Data", "Save Data", condition=lambda state: state["processed_data"] is not None)
```

---

4. Method: run

Executes the workflow, starting from nodes with no incoming edges (or explicitly defined start nodes).

Signature:

python

```
run(state: dict = None)
```

- **state**: An optional dictionary to pass shared data between nodes.

Example:

python

```python
state = {"data": [1, 2, 3]}
graph.run(state=state)
```

5. Conditional Execution

Conditions allow workflows to branch dynamically based on the state.

Example:

python

```python
def check_condition(state):
    return state["processed_data"] is not None

graph.add_edge("Process Data", "Save Data", condition=check_condition)
```

Example: Comprehensive Workflow Using LangGraph

Scenario: Data Processing Workflow

A workflow that:

1. Validates input data.
2. Processes data if valid.
3. Saves results to storage.

Code:

python

```python
from langgraph import LangGraph

# Define functions
def validate_data(state):
    state["is_valid"] = all(isinstance(x, int) for x in state["data"])
    print(f"Data validation result: {state['is_valid']}")
```

```python
    return state

def process_data(state):
    if state["is_valid"]:
        state["processed_data"] = [x * 2 for x in state["data"]]
        print(f"Processed data: {state['processed_data']}")
    return state

def save_data(state):
    if "processed_data" in state:
        print(f"Saving data: {state['processed_data']}")
    else:
        print("No data to save.")
    return state

# Create LangGraph instance
graph = LangGraph()
graph.add_node("Validate Data", function=validate_data)
graph.add_node("Process Data", function=process_data)
graph.add_node("Save Data", function=save_data)

# Define workflow
graph.add_edge("Validate Data", "Process Data", condition=lambda state: state["is_valid"])
graph.add_edge("Process Data", "Save Data")

# Execute workflow
state = {"data": [1, 2, 3]}
graph.run(state=state)
```

Output:

plaintext

Data validation result: True

Processed data: [2, 4, 6]

Saving data: [2, 4, 6]

API Reference Table

Method	Description	Example
add_node	Adds a task or function to the workflow.	graph.add_node("Task A", function=task_function)
add_edge	Creates a connection between nodes to define execution order.	graph.add_edge("Task A", "Task B")
run	Executes the workflow from the starting node(s).	graph.run(state=workflow_state)
condition	Allows conditional execution of edges based on workflow state.	graph.add_edge("Task A", "Task B", condition=lambda state: state["value"] > 10)
state	Shared data structure for passing information between nodes.	state = {"key": "value"}

Summary

In this appendix, we covered:

1. **Detailed LangGraph API Documentation**:
    - Overview of methods, their signatures, and usage.
2. **Key Classes and Methods Explained**:

- Examples of add_node, add_edge, and run.

3. **Comprehensive Workflow Example**:
    - A real-world scenario demonstrating the LangGraph API.

LangGraph's API is designed to be intuitive and powerful, enabling developers to model and execute complex workflows with minimal effort. For further reference, consult the official LangGraph documentation or experiment with custom workflows to deepen your understanding. Let me know if you'd like additional details or examples!

Appendix B: Glossary of Terms

This appendix provides definitions of core concepts and terminology related to LangGraph, LangChain, and Multi-agent AI. It serves as a quick reference guide to help readers understand the technical terms and concepts used throughout the book.

B.1 Definitions of Core Concepts

1. Agent

- **Definition**: An autonomous entity that performs specific tasks or decisions within a system, often based on predefined rules or AI models.
- **Example**: A chatbot agent that handles customer queries.

2. Workflow

- **Definition**: A sequence of connected tasks or processes designed to achieve a specific goal.
- **Example**: A data processing workflow might include tasks for validation, transformation, and storage.

3. Node

- **Definition**: A single task or function within a workflow. In LangGraph, nodes represent distinct computational units.
- **Example**: A node might process user data or call an external API.

4. Edge

- **Definition**: A connection between nodes that defines the execution order of tasks in a workflow.
- **Example**: An edge connects the "Process Data" node to the "Save Results" node.

5. **State**
    - **Definition**: A shared data structure that nodes in a workflow can access and modify to pass information.
    - **Example**: A workflow's state might store the results of a data validation task for use by subsequent nodes.

6. **Conditional Execution**
    - **Definition**: The ability to execute certain nodes or edges in a workflow based on specific conditions or states.
    - **Example**: A workflow might skip a node if the input data fails validation.

7. **Persistence**
    - **Definition**: The capability to save and resume workflows, retaining their state across sessions.
    - **Example**: Saving the state of a partially completed workflow for resumption after a system restart.

8. **Orchestration**
    - **Definition**: The process of coordinating and managing the execution of multiple workflows or tasks.
    - **Example**: A workflow orchestrating data ingestion, analysis, and reporting.

B.2 Terminology Related to LangChain and Multi-agent AI

1. **LangChain**
    - **Definition**: A framework designed to build applications powered by Large Language Models (LLMs) with tools for chaining prompts, handling memory, and connecting external tools.

- **Example**: LangChain can be used to create a question-answering system that fetches data from a database.

2. Multi-Agent System

- **Definition**: A system where multiple autonomous agents interact to solve complex problems collaboratively.
- **Example**: A customer support system with agents for handling queries, routing tickets, and analyzing feedback.

3. Agentic AI

- **Definition**: AI systems that demonstrate autonomous behavior, making decisions and taking actions to achieve goals.
- **Example**: A trading bot that analyzes market data and makes trades without human intervention.

4. Large Language Model (LLM)

- **Definition**: A machine learning model trained on extensive text data to perform tasks like text generation, summarization, and question answering.
- **Example**: OpenAI's GPT models.

5. Embedding

- **Definition**: A numerical representation of data (e.g., text or images) in a lower-dimensional space, often used for similarity searches.
- **Example**: An embedding can represent a word or sentence for input into an LLM.

6. Prompt Engineering

- **Definition**: The process of crafting effective inputs (prompts) to guide the behavior of an AI model.
- **Example**: Providing detailed instructions to an LLM to generate accurate summaries.

7. Intent Recognition

- **Definition**: Identifying the purpose or goal of a user's input in conversational AI systems.
- **Example**: Recognizing "I want to track my order" as an intent for tracking a shipment.

8. Knowledge Graph

- **Definition**: A structured representation of knowledge as entities and their relationships, enabling semantic searches and reasoning.
- **Example**: A knowledge graph might store information about movies, actors, and genres for a recommendation system.

9. Hyperautomation

- **Definition**: The integration of multiple technologies like AI, RPA (Robotic Process Automation), and IoT to automate end-to-end business processes.
- **Example**: Automating an entire customer onboarding process, from document collection to account creation.

10. Token

- **Definition**: A unit of text (word, subword, or character) used in natural language processing.
- **Example**: The phrase "LangGraph is powerful" consists of three tokens.

11. Context Window

- **Definition**: The amount of text a language model can process or consider at once.
- **Example**: A model with a 4,000-token context window can analyze up to 4,000 tokens of input and output combined.

12. Streaming Output

- **Definition**: Incremental generation of output by an AI model, delivering data in real-time instead of waiting for full completion.

- **Example**: Streaming sentences as they are generated in a chatbot conversation.

13. API Integration

- **Definition**: Connecting workflows to external systems via Application Programming Interfaces (APIs) for data exchange or functionality.
- **Example**: Using an API to fetch live weather data in a LangGraph workflow.

14. Conditional Logic

- **Definition**: Rules that dictate workflow behavior based on specific conditions.
- **Example**: Sending a notification only if a task exceeds its deadline.

15. Observability

- **Definition**: The ability to monitor and understand the behavior and performance of workflows through metrics, logs, and traces.
- **Example**: Using Prometheus and Grafana to track workflow execution time and error rates.

Glossary Summary Table

Term	Definition
Agent	Autonomous entity performing specific tasks.
Workflow	A sequence of tasks aimed at achieving a goal.
Node	A task or function within a workflow.
Edge	A connection defining task execution order.
State	Shared data accessible by nodes.
Conditional	Execution of nodes based on specific

Term	Definition
Execution	conditions.
Persistence	Saving and resuming workflows.
Orchestration	Coordinating multiple workflows.
LangChain	Framework for building LLM-based applications.
Multi-Agent System	Collaborative system of multiple agents.
Agentic AI	AI systems with autonomous decision-making capabilities.
Large Language Model	AI model trained on vast text data.
Embedding	Numerical representation of data for machine learning tasks.
Prompt Engineering	Designing effective inputs for AI models.
Intent Recognition	Identifying the purpose of user input in conversational systems.
Knowledge Graph	Structured representation of entities and their relationships.
Hyperautomation	End-to-end automation using multiple technologies.
Token	A unit of text in natural language processing.
Context Window	The amount of text a model can process at once.
Streaming Output	Incremental, real-time output generation.
API Integration	Connecting workflows to external systems via APIs.

Term	Definition
Conditional Logic	Rules guiding workflow behavior.
Observability	Monitoring and understanding workflow performance.

Summary

This chapter defined key terms and concepts related to LangGraph, LangChain, and multi-agent AI systems. These definitions provide clarity for readers, ensuring they understand the technical language used throughout the book. Let me know if you'd like to add or expand any specific terms!

Appendix C: Troubleshooting Guide

This troubleshooting guide is designed to help LangGraph users identify, diagnose, and resolve common issues. It also includes frequently asked questions (FAQs) to address common user concerns and provide clarity on various features and functionalities.

C.1 Common Issues and Resolutions

1. Workflow Execution Fails Unexpectedly

- **Cause**: Missing or incorrectly configured nodes or edges.
- **Symptoms**:
    - Error messages indicating missing nodes or unconnected edges.
    - Workflow terminates without completing.
- **Resolution**:
    - Verify that all nodes are connected using the add_edge method.
    - Use visualization tools to inspect the workflow structure.

Example:

python

```
graph.add_edge("Start", "End")  # Ensure all nodes are connected
```

Debugging Tip: Visualize the workflow structure with a library like NetworkX:

python

```python
import networkx as nx
import matplotlib.pyplot as plt

# Visualize graph structure
graph = nx.DiGraph()
graph.add_edge("Start", "Process Data")
graph.add_edge("Process Data", "End")

nx.draw(graph, with_labels=True, node_color="lightblue")
plt.show()
```

2. Incorrect Data Passed Between Nodes

- **Cause**: Mismanagement of the state object.
- **Symptoms**:
    - Errors like KeyError or TypeError.
    - Unexpected or missing outputs from nodes.
- **Resolution**:
    - Validate the data structure at each node.
    - Add checks to ensure keys exist before accessing them.

Example:

python

```python
def process_data(state):
    if "data" not in state:
        raise KeyError("Missing 'data' in state")
    state["processed_data"] = [x * 2 for x in state["data"]]
    return state
```

3. Conditional Edges Not Working as Expected

- **Cause**: Incorrect logic in the condition function.

- **Symptoms**:
    - Nodes execute when they shouldn't, or fail to execute when they should.
- **Resolution**:
    - Test the condition function independently.
    - Ensure the function returns a Boolean value (True or False).

Example:

python

```
graph.add_edge("Validate Data", "Process Data", condition=lambda state: state.get("is_valid", False))
```

4. Workflow Runs Too Slowly

- **Cause**: Inefficient node functions or lack of parallel execution.
- **Symptoms**:
    - Long runtime for workflows with multiple nodes.
- **Resolution**:
    - Optimize node functions by reducing computational overhead.
    - Use parallel execution for independent tasks.

Example: Enable parallel execution with LangGraph:

python

```
graph.run(parallel=True)
```

5. Error Messages Lack Context

- **Cause**: Insufficient logging or error handling.
- **Symptoms**:
    - Generic error messages that don't specify the failing node or issue.
- **Resolution**:
    - Add detailed logging to each node function.
    - Include exception handling for common errors.

Example:

python

```
import logging

logging.basicConfig(level=logging.INFO)

def process_node(state):
    try:
        # Simulate processing
        state["result"] = 10 / state["divider"]
    except ZeroDivisionError:
        logging.error("Division by zero error in process_node")
        state["result"] = None
    return state
```

---

6. Workflow Hangs or Stalls

- **Cause**: Cyclic dependencies or long-running tasks without timeout.
- **Symptoms**:
    - Workflow doesn't complete.
- **Resolution**:
    - Check for cyclic dependencies in the graph.

- Use timeouts or asynchronous execution for long-running tasks.

Debugging Tip: Use a cycle detection algorithm to identify loops:

python

```
if nx.find_cycle(graph):
    print("Cycle detected in the workflow")
```

C.2 FAQs for LangGraph Users

1. How do I debug a failing workflow?

- Use the following steps:
    1. **Inspect the state object**: Log its content at each node.
    2. **Visualize the workflow**: Ensure all nodes are connected.
    3. **Check for cyclic dependencies**: Use tools like NetworkX.

2. Can I use external APIs in my workflow?

- Yes, you can integrate external APIs by calling them within node functions.

Example:

python

```
import requests

def fetch_data(state):
    response = requests.get("https://api.example.com/data")
```

```python
    if response.status_code == 200:
        state["api_data"] = response.json()
    else:
        raise Exception("Failed to fetch data from API")
    return state
```

3. How do I handle errors gracefully?

- Add exception handling in node functions and use fallback nodes for critical tasks.

Example:

python

```python
def fallback_node(state):
    print("Executing fallback logic...")
    return state
```

```python
graph.add_edge("Main Task", "Fallback Node", condition=lambda state: state.get("error"))
```

4. How do I improve workflow performance?

- Use these strategies:
    - Optimize individual node functions.
    - Parallelize independent tasks.
    - Implement caching for reusable data.

5. Can I pause and resume workflows?

- Yes, LangGraph supports persistence. Save the state object and reload it to resume execution.

6. **What are the best practices for designing workflows?**

    - **Modularize**: Break workflows into reusable components.

    - **Validate Data**: Ensure inputs and outputs match expected formats.

    - **Log**: Add logging to track workflow execution.

Summary

In this appendix, we covered:

1. **Common Issues and Resolutions**:

    - Addressing execution failures, data issues, and performance bottlenecks.

2. **FAQs for LangGraph Users**:

    - Providing answers to common user concerns.

This guide is designed to empower LangGraph users to troubleshoot efficiently and build robust workflows. For additional support, refer to the official documentation or user community forums. Let me know if you'd like further clarification or more examples!

Appendix D: Online Resources and Community Support

D.1 Links to Tutorials and Code Repositories

Official Documentation

- The official LangGraph documentation is the best starting point for understanding its features, API, and best practices.
    - **URL**: LangGraph Documentation *(Placeholder URL)*

Tutorials and Guides

1. **Beginner-Friendly Tutorials**:
    - Step-by-step guides on setting up and using LangGraph for simple workflows.
    - **Example**: "Your First LangGraph Workflow"
        - Learn to create a basic workflow with nodes, edges, and state management.
        - **URL**: LangGraph Basics Tutorial *(Placeholder URL)*

2. **Advanced Use Cases**:
    - In-depth guides on implementing advanced features like conditional logic, parallel execution, and API integrations.
    - **Example**: "Building Scalable Multi-Agent Systems"
        - **URL**: LangGraph Advanced Guide *(Placeholder URL)*

3. **Video Tutorials**:
    - Watch demonstrations of LangGraph workflows in action.
    - **Example**: "Visual Debugging with LangGraph"
        - **URL**: LangGraph Video Tutorials *(Placeholder URL)*

Code Repositories

1. **Official GitHub Repository**:
    - Access the LangGraph source code, examples, and sample projects.
    - **URL**: LangGraph GitHub *(Placeholder URL)*

2. **Community-Contributed Examples**:
    - Explore workflows shared by the community, including use cases for:
        - Data pipelines
        - Multi-agent systems
        - Real-time processing
    - **URL**: Community Examples *(Placeholder URL)*

3. **Template Projects**:
    - Prebuilt templates to jumpstart projects:
        - Chatbot frameworks
        - Data processing workflows
    - **URL**: LangGraph Templates *(Placeholder URL)*

Blogs and Articles

1. **LangGraph Blog**:

- Regularly updated articles on new features, case studies, and industry insights.
- **URL**: LangGraph Blog *(Placeholder URL)*

2. **Developer Tutorials**:
   - Tutorials and tips from LangGraph experts.
   - **URL**: LangGraph Tutorials *(Placeholder URL)*

D.2 Community Forums and Discussion Groups

Official LangGraph Forum

- A dedicated platform for asking questions, sharing knowledge, and discussing ideas.
  - **Features**:
    - Categorized topics (e.g., beginner questions, advanced usage, bug reports).
    - Moderated by LangGraph developers.
  - **URL**: LangGraph Forum *(Placeholder URL)*

Discussion Groups

1. **Slack Community**:
   - Real-time communication for troubleshooting and networking.
   - **URL**: LangGraph Slack *(Placeholder URL)*
2. **Reddit**:
   - Join the LangGraph subreddit for informal discussions and tips.

- **URL:** LangGraph Subreddit *(Placeholder URL)*

3. **Discord Server:**
    - Engage with a vibrant community of developers working on LangGraph projects.
    - **URL:** LangGraph Discord *(Placeholder URL)*

Social Media Platforms

1. **Twitter:**
    - Follow updates, announcements, and quick tips.
    - **Handle:** @LangGraphAI *(Placeholder URL)*
2. **LinkedIn Group:**
    - Connect with professionals using LangGraph in various industries.
    - **URL:** LangGraph LinkedIn *(Placeholder URL)*

D.3 Staying Updated on LangGraph Developments

Newsletter Subscription

- Receive regular updates on:
    - New releases
    - Feature announcements
    - Upcoming events and webinars
- **Sign Up:** LangGraph Newsletter *(Placeholder URL)*

GitHub Release Notifications

- Subscribe to the LangGraph repository on GitHub to track updates and releases.

    - **How To**:

        1. Go to the LangGraph GitHub Page *(Placeholder URL)*.

        2. Click "Watch" and select "Releases only."

Conferences and Meetups

- Attend events to learn from experts and network with other LangGraph users.

    - **LangGraph Summit**:

        - An annual conference showcasing the latest innovations.

        - **Details**: LangGraph Summit *(Placeholder URL)*

Contributing to LangGraph

- Join the LangGraph open-source community to contribute code, report issues, or suggest new features.

    - **How To Get Involved**:

        - Submit pull requests on GitHub.

        - Participate in community discussions.

Resource Table

Resource Type	Description	URL
Official Documentation	Comprehensive guide to LangGraph's API and features.	LangGraph Docs
Tutorials	Step-by-step guides for beginners and advanced users.	LangGraph Tutorials
GitHub Repository	Source code and community-contributed examples.	LangGraph GitHub
Blog	Insights, case studies, and industry updates.	LangGraph Blog
Community Forum	Q&A platform for developers and users.	LangGraph Forum
Slack	Real-time communication with the LangGraph community.	LangGraph Slack
Discord	Networking and informal discussions.	LangGraph Discord
Newsletter	Updates on new releases, events, and features.	LangGraph Newsletter

Summary

This appendix provides a detailed list of resources for learning, troubleshooting, and collaborating with the LangGraph community. From official documentation and tutorials to discussion forums and social media groups, these resources will empower users to deepen their understanding of LangGraph and stay updated on the latest developments. Let me know if you'd like to expand on any specific resource or include additional links!

www.ingramcontent.com/pod-product-compliance
Lightning Source LLC
Chambersburg PA
CBHW082247220526
45469CB00009B/2902